Stages

Onion River Press
89 Church Street
Burlington, VT 05401
info@onionriverpress.com / www.onionriverpress.com
ISBN: 978-1-957184-89-0
Library of Congress Control Number: 2024922940

Cover and Book Design by Tina Christensen
Cover Art and Interior Illustrations by Lorraine Halpin Zaloom

Stages

Ruminations, Rants, and Reminiscences
on a Life in Music

Paul Asbell

ONION
RIVER

PRESS

Burlington, Vermont

Contents

Victor Hugo

Preface

*"Music expresses that which cannot be said,
and on which it is impossible to be silent."*

That thought, so perfectly expressed by Victor Hugo, is at the heart of my life's work. However, from time to time, I've put virtual pen to virtual paper, in hopes of expressing some of the things that words CAN say. And, occasionally, some things on which it was impossible to be silent.

I've been writing essays from time to time, reminiscing on my upbringing in a musical family, the Chicago blues scene I was lucky enough to be part of, and the wonderful men (and occasionally women) who I worked with there. In these essays, I've occasionally indulged in various ruminations about how music exposes us to deeper truths about the world we live in. On somewhat rarer occasions, I've allowed myself to speculate on how the world we live in could be a whole lot better than it is presently.

From time to time, as people waxed complimentary about this piece or the other, the chorus "So when's the book coming out?" got started. I would generally reply that "I've already taken on one questionably profitable artistic endeavor for this lifetime. I hardly need take on another."

And besides. Having an author for a father makes one a bit reticent—gun-shy, even?—about following in the old man's footsteps.

Still, the appreciation for a well-turned phrase has turned out to be a hard jones to kick. And, as so often happens to people in my chosen profession, what began innocently enough as occasional dabbling has now turned into a full-blown habit. A habit which compels me to try to put into words some of the competing feelings of joy and regret, of pride and self-doubt, of admiration and disappointment, and of ambivalence and firm resolve, which my musical endeavors have awakened and cultivated in me over the 65+ years I've been doing it.

So, now, resistance having proven futile, I'd like to express my gratitude to the chorus of readers who've persisted in encouraging me to fashion these ruminations, rants, and reminiscences into book form. Many of you know who you are, and I thank you all!

A quick note on what this book is. And perhaps more importantly—and certainly easier to describe—what it ISN'T.

This book is not, nor is it intended to be, a scholarly history of the music or the musicians I've had the privilege of working with and getting to know. I have many friends who specialize in that field and have produced excellent work, which I highly recommend. Since this book does not aim to provide such an exhaustive study, I've included recommendations in the appendix for books and other resources that curious readers can explore for a more in-depth, comprehensive dive.

What this book DOES try to offer is a highly personalized peek into the world I grew up in. One in which musicians performed in a far more local, less media-driven, more "real-time" and less "virtual" setting than the way music is experienced today, in the internet-saturated world we presently live in. For better or for worse, that "analog" world that existed 60 years ago is largely gone, never to return.

Ironically, however, our highly technological world provides all sorts of opportunities to create "multi-media" presentations in which it's possible to experience the music being described, or view images of the performers, while reading the stories. To that end, I've tried whenever possible to use QR codes to link to YouTube recordings relating to the artists discussed. I suspect that a reading of this book, with one hand cradling an iPad or iPhone, would be a fine way to immerse oneself in the world I've attempted to capture in my essays.

This book wouldn't have been possible without the encouragement, advice, support, suggestions, and keen punctuational eyes of many people. I'd particularly like to thank David Ziegele, Mark Hoffman, Kim Field, Dick Shurman, Jodi

Asbell-Clarke, Dave Cavanagh, Bill Schubart, Steve Blodgett, Bob Recupero, Casey Dennis, and Riley Earle for their assistance in shaping and perfecting the stories, and influencing the overall arc of this book.

I'd also like to thank Tina Christensen and Lorraine Halpin Zaloom for their fine work in adding so much to the visual component of these stories.

And finally, huge thanks to Bill Berg, for his huge help in "paying it forward" and making this project possible.

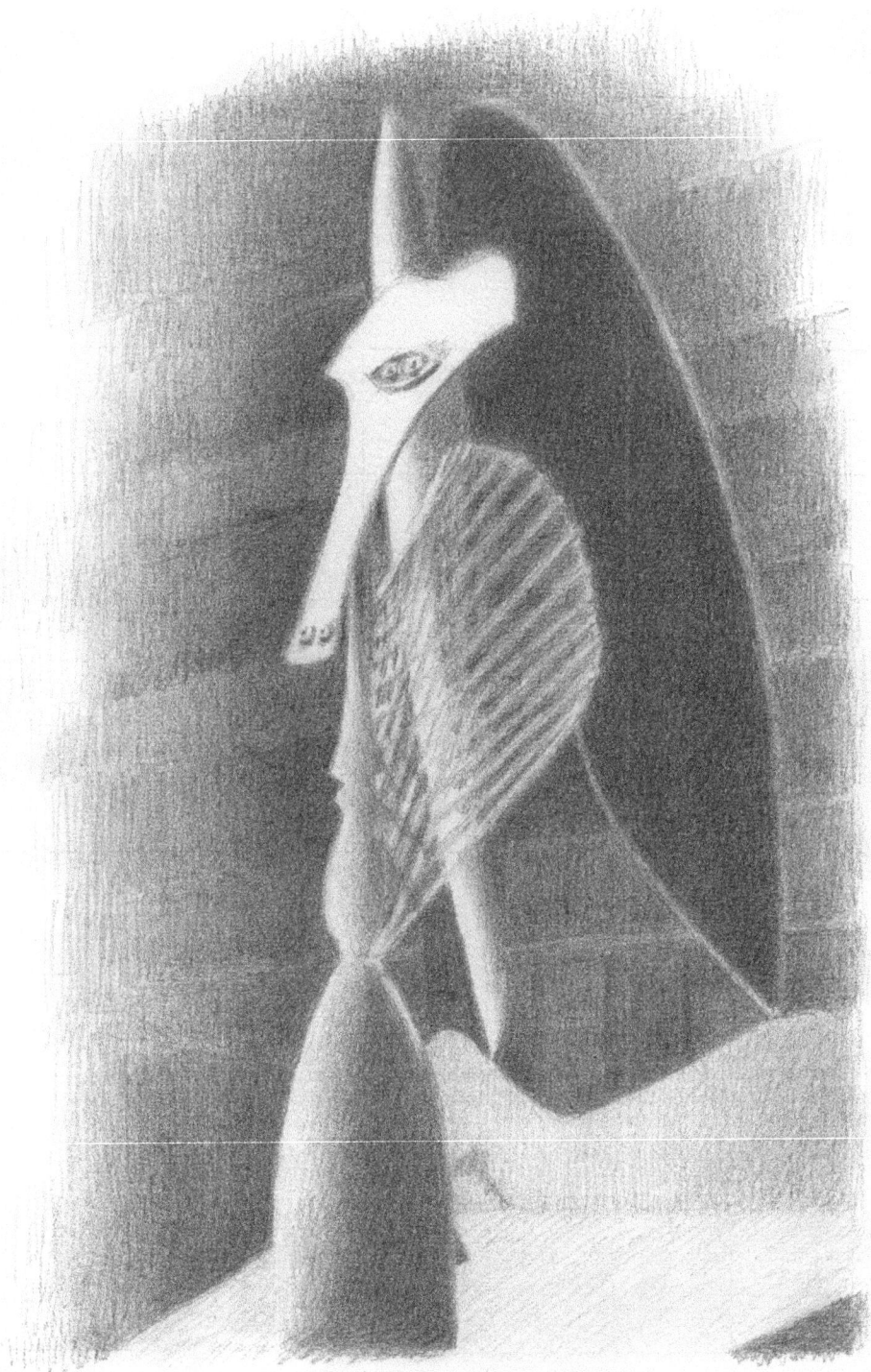

Picasso Sculpture, Daley Plaza, Chicago

Rich Men, and a Rich Man's Woman

The first few months of 1968 found me living in a dingy apartment on my hometown of Chicago's South Side, along with two guys I had befriended during freshman year at University of Chicago. While Peter and David were in their second year at UC, I had dropped out after a revelatory trip to Mexico over Christmas break, which had depleted the money I had saved for expenses for spring term. As a result, I was forced to take a day gig as a messenger boy for the now-extinct accounting firm Arthur Andersen, whose skyscraper-size office building was located in Daley Plaza, opposite the freshly installed Picasso sculpture in Chicago's business district, known as "the Loop." At night, I was playing blues clubs on the South and West Side, making $22 a night, working alongside men two and three times my age, and learning musical and personal skills which I still use to this day.

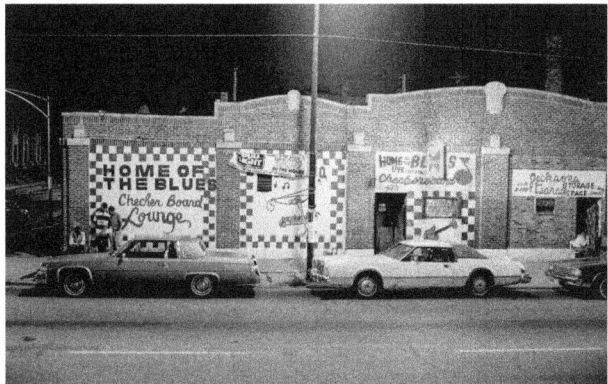

Checkerboard Lounge, Chicago

The Arthur Andersen gig (the first and last "straight job" I ever worked) involved getting up way earlier than my lifestyle allowed, taking the "IC" train downtown, punching in to the office, and then spending the day running errands around the sprawling Chicago metro area. As a result, I learned a lot about the layout of the city, and neighborhoods other than the South Side ones I grew up in.

I also learned a lot about the side hustles that other messenger boys at the firm were using to augment their meager salaries. One of those hustles involved travel receipts. Messenger boys were instructed to take cabs to and from our destinations, and then hand in cabbie receipts, in order to get reimbursed by the firm. But I quickly learned that in return for a generous tip, a cabbie could be persuaded to part with a fistful of blank receipts—enabling me to take cheaper public transit to and from the destination and forge a cab receipt for reimbursement.

After a few weeks of mastering the finer points of this low-level grift, I discovered another additional benefit, which—when combined with my growing passion for the music I played at night in the clubs—became a powerful synergy of motivation.

While walking from the "L" stop to my destination, I stumbled upon dozens of small record shops, many of which contained hard-to-find records of artists I needed to bone up on. (In the era of YouTube, Pandora, Google and file-sharing, it's hard to describe the "holy grail" search that blues fans once made in order to actually hear the music of then-obscure artists like Robert Nighthawk, Doctor Clayton, Baby Face Leroy, Earl Hooker, and countless others whom we only knew from reading the liner notes of out-of-print LPs.)

Thanks to my enthusiastic pawings through the dusty bins of these record shops, I learned the names of dozens of fly-by-night record labels who released music by the lesser-known blues artists I was searching out. Labels like Cuca, Parkway, Chief, and USA soon became the focus of my quest. Of course, I was already well-familiar with the output of Chess—the preeminent Chicago label—so when I found a 45 by Muddy Waters from 1965 that I had never heard before on any of my LPs, I eagerly snapped it up and took it home to listen to later.

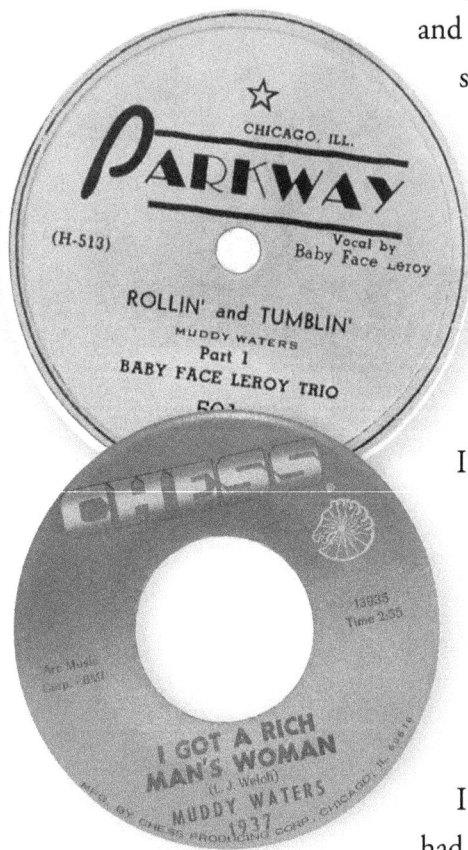

The song was called "I've Got a Rich Man's Woman," and now that YouTube resides on literally everyone's computers, it's a simple thing to look it up, listen, and enjoy.

Record Store, 35th and Giles, Chicago

Thanks to my friend in the blues, Tom Morris, for reminding me recently of this great Chess track. Now, listening to it after 55+ years of recording experience, I hear something that never occurred to me as a younger fan. The great vocal cadenza that Mud tagged onto the end of his tune—as he often did in live performance—is absolutely identical in every respect to the beginning of the tune. Meaning that it must've impressed someone so much that they asked engineer Malcolm Chisholm to figure out a way to copy the tape and splice it onto the beginning as well.

Behold, the magic of production… a topic which I explore in greater depth in the chapter entitled "Puppet Shows, and The Producer" and "'The London Howlin' Wolf Sessions,' and Sausage-Making."

Muddy Waters

But let's return to my "on-the-job training" at Arthur Andersen. Anyone who remembers the Enron scandal of 2001 will recall that the high-level grift of CEO Ken Lay and others ultimately brought down both the Texas energy giant and their once-mighty accounting firm, Arthur Andersen. As I think back on my low-level side hustles while in the firm's employ, I suspect I was I simply channeling a company-wide climate of overall corruption. At least, that's my story 55+ years later—and I'm stickin' to it.

If my "channeling" story is indeed correct, then I'll offer the further observation that the brief time I spent honing my grifting skills in the corrupt corporate world of Arthur Andersen ironically foreshadowed my longer stay in the Chicago blues world.

In both cases, I was fortunate enough to be mentored by the very best in the biz.

★ BENEFIT CONCERT FOR ★
☞ BIG BILL BROONZY ☜

FEATURING
MAHALIA JACKSON!

★★ PETE ★★
SEEGER

BLUES SINGERS
MUDDY WATERS
EDDIE BOYD | **LITTLE WALTER**
MEMPHIS SLIM | **SUNNYLAND SLIM**

FOLK SINGERS
Gerry Armstrong
FLEMING BROWN
Bernie Asbell
FRANK HAMILTON ★ LARRY LANE
AND OTHERS!!!

WED. NOV. 27
EVE.

8:30 P. M. ❦ DONATION $2.00

KAM TEMPLE, 930 E. 50TH ST.

MAIL ORDERS: Big Bill Broonzy, 1450 S. Karlov Ave., Chicago 23
please enclose stamped self addressed envelope

A Benefit Concert, On a School Night

Those of us "of a certain age" will remember the experience of poring through cardboard boxes full of memorabilia relating to our parents and finding a fascinating tidbit from their early life. (For a deeper dive into this topic, see my "Cardboard Boxes, and Origin Stories" piece later in the book.) Thanks to my old friend Rik Palieri, I recently experienced the digital equivalent.

This poster, which I had never seen before, is of an event that took place on November 27, 1957, when I was eight years old. The image ties together so many disparate pieces of my own life that my mind raced as I reflected on all the connections.

The event itself was a benefit to offset blues singer and guitarist Bill Broonzy's medical expenses, due to his ailing health. Bill was a friend of my parents, and I suspect my dad—in addition to performing on the program—may have been an organizer of the event, since the event's location, KAM Temple, was around two blocks from our house on 50th Street. (A few years later, after asking my mother why we didn't go to temple like my cousins' family, I briefly attended KAM myself. That short-lived experiment ended after a friend explained that the objective of attendance—something called a "Bar Mitzvah"—involved studying Hebrew in Sunday School for a year and half, and then receiving around $1,500 in gifts. When it was pointed out that a substantial percentage of those gifts would be in the form of "Cedars of Lebanon" bonds, I decided that the numbers wouldn't work for me and left Sunday school soon after. But that's another story, for another time …)

Bill Broonzy, 1930s

Many years later, in my teens, I became serious about learning to play the blues guitar styles I was listening to on recordings from the '30s. By that time, I was beginning to realize that the Bill Broonzy who I was hearing perform virtuosic instrumentals and sophisticated studio session accompaniments—and singing racy, double-entendre "party blues"—was the same guy whose politically topical, down-home "folk-blues" I had heard around the house growing up. I also realized that, like many people, my mom had no idea of Bill's earlier, racier musical career and his subsequent re-invention—nor was she especially pleased by the notion. It was an early eye-opener for me about the complexities of the professional world … especially in the music biz.

The concert's headliner, Mahalia Jackson, had by then been hailed as "the world's greatest gospel singer"—a billing which implied that her name might actually be recognizable to mainstream popular culture in the U.S. (and thus earning her the exclamation point on the poster!). A few months before this benefit concert, she had appeared at the Newport Jazz Festival, widening her exposure to white audiences. Her records had been in continual rotation in my parents' home while growing up, and I remember seeing her sing in several South Side churches, which I visited with my dad. Those early Black church visits—and the awareness that the music itself was only a part of the total experience—have stayed with me all my life.

Pete Seeger had been a longtime friend of each of my parents since the early '40s. My dad first met Pete in Greenwich Village, at informal gatherings that eventually coalesced as a group called "People's Songs," and concertized with him often after that. My mom knew Pete separately from her work promoting liberal causes during the days when she worked in Washington D.C. In 1946, after getting married, my mom and dad moved to Chicago to open the midwest chapter of People's Songs (more on this move in my story "Cardboard Boxes, and Origin Stories.")

Pete was a frequent visitor to the house during those years; so when Pete (along with my dad and many others) was blacklisted during the McCarthy era of the early '50s, my mom concocted a plan for Pete to get bookings in pre-schools and similar events as a small source of income. I chuckle now to think how many youthful minds were poisoned by Pete's infectious singalongs as a result of my mom's subversive promotions!

The name Muddy Waters is an iconic one by now, and his image is celebrated everywhere in our culture—from block-long urban mural-scapes to hip coffeehouses. But during the mid-'50s, his music was not especially beloved by most white audiences. When I was hired to play on Muddy's now-legendary *Fathers and Sons* recording in April 1969, I called home to pass on the great news. I recall my mom appearing somewhat less than thrilled to hear about my career accomplishment. When I asked about her demeanor, she surprised me by referring to Muddy in rather disapproving terms. When I pressed a bit further, she explained her view of Muddy as one of the new breed of Chicago blues singers whose success with Black audiences signaled the obsolescence of her friend Bill Broonzy's older, more "authentic" style of blues, and ultimately marked the end of his career. Another eye-opener for me—that the concept of authenticity is in the eye of the beholder, and is subject to constant generational redefinition.

Although Fleming Brown is far less known, his name on the poster jumped out at me as my dad's regular concertizing partner for several years. I still remember trying to go to

Muddy Waters mural, State Street, Chicago

sleep on school nights, kept awake by the strident sound of his banjo while he and my dad played together downstairs in the living room. Only now am I reflecting that they were not just "playing," but rehearsing for performances like the one at this benefit concert.

Little Walter, Eddie Boyd, Memphis Slim—all names of people I saw perform 10 to 12 years after this show. But, of course, I'm now wondering if I might actually have been AT this show, held right down the street from my house! Would I have remembered it, at eight years old? Maybe not.

Another eye-opener, about which childhood events we consider significant enough to remember, and which just become noise from downstairs, that keep you awake on a school night.

Alley Oop In The Ozarks

The first record that I bought with my own money was a 45RPM single, which I acquired when I was 9 years old. Though I grew up in inner-city Chicago, the actual purchase took place in the little town of Mountain View, in the red-dirt heart of rural Arkansas. My family had taken a trip there so that my dad could interview a songwriter named Jimmy Driftwood for a magazine article he had been hired to write.

While dad and mom were staying at the Driftwood's cabin in Timbo, my brothers and I were placed in a horse camp in the nearby town of Mountain View, where I was freaked out by campfire stories of water moccasins and the prospect of using the smelly, communal outhouse for a week. (I learned, among other things, that you can't go for two weeks without making #2 ... but more about that later, in my story "Arkansas Travelers".)

Anyway, in my occasional trips to town, I heard a song on the jukebox of a local cafe that my friends and I were not supposed to go into. The tune sounded fantastic to my 9-year-old ears. Its name was easy to remember because the refrain repeated constantly. "Alley Oop ... Oop ... Oop-Oop." I had heard vibey, "street-sounding" music like it back home in Chicago, but this tune had a Flintstones-cartoon aspect that made it even better.

I had saved enough allowances to buy the 45...but didn't know how one went about doing that. My friends at the horse camp directed me to a local hardware store—which was where one bought such things in Mountain View, Arkansas—and there I bought my first-ever, very-own record.

When I brought the 45 home and played it, though, I experienced the first in a lifetime of subtle letdowns; the feeling of listening to my own record—in my own home—was not as thrilling as listening to it on the jukebox in that cafe in Mountain View.

A profound realization, and the first in a lifetime of similar epiphanies about place, and time, and emotional context.

However, as I found out later, there was also a more mundane explanation for my feeling of disappointment.

The original version I heard in the cafe was by a hastily thrown-together doo-wop group from Los Angeles that called themselves the Hollywood Argyles. But unbeknownst to me, the copy that I had bought at the hardware store was by a "cover group" called Dante and the Evergreens. The song, the words, the arrangement, and the goofiness were the same, but the vibe was a bit less edgy, somehow more antiseptic—as the producers no doubt intended, to appeal better to young, mainstream audiences.

But the "bait n' switch" tactic didn't work for me. I was indignant when I realized how it all worked, and have spent the better part of a musical lifetime trying not to confuse the "cover" with the "real deal!"

My California

When I was twelve, I started to pore through a bunch of old 78 records that my dad kept in the back of a record cabinet in our living room. There was all sorts of music on them—all completely different than the songs I was hearing on the little radio I had recently built in my bedroom from a Heathkit.

There was a scratchy-sounding recording of a guy named Blind Willie Johnson, who sang in a raspy voice while echoing his words with a spooky guitar style that I later found out was the result of using a pocketknife over the strings—a style that would eventually become commonplace when performed by guitarists using a bottleneck, socket wrench, or pill bottle. There was a group called the Carter Family, whose old-time country singing and playing reminded me of the recordings of Woody Guthrie, a friend of my dad's (I later found out WHY I was so reminded—Woody had listened to Carter Family 78s himself as a youngster, and "borrowed" many of their melodies to mate with his own politically-inspired lyrics). And in a similar vein to my ears, there was a guy named Uncle Dave Macon, who played banjo in a raucous style while singing in a voice that struck me as a cross between Walter Brennan and W.C. Fields.

Each time I put the needle down (carefully!) on one of these records, I entered a time/space warp that instantly transported me to the place where I could imagine the music lived. Each one of those places felt quite real to me—at least, for the three-or-so minutes that the song lasted. But as soon as the needle reached that last groove, and the song ended, the scratchy sound that followed jolted me right back to 1962 and my parents' living room.

I longed to find—on my own guitar—those notes and timbres that might allow me to enter that time/space warp, like those records did. But my attempts to transport myself out of my living room—and enter that place where the music lived—seemed to resist all my early efforts. There was, however, one record that hinted at the possibility of breaking through. The song was called "My California" by a guy from Houston, Texas named Lightnin' Hopkins. For some reason, the sound of those very first guitar notes on that scratchy record seemed to awaken a sense of recognition within me—a sense that these were notes that I could decode, find on my guitar, and learn to reproduce myself.

Lightnin's first spoken words on the record, "Here's that California Blues … ," reminded me of the Dust Bowl Ballads of Woody Guthrie, which I had grown up listening to on that record player of my dad's. Those songs of Woody's had already burned into my brain a vivid soundscape of Oklahoma farm country, where a family man wistfully dreams of a faraway land filled with milk and honey, where dust storms never blow. A surreptitious late-night viewing of the movie version of John Steinbeck's novel *Grapes of Wrath* provided the perfect black-and-white visual image needed to accompany the spartan tones of Woody's guitar and his flat Okie accent and singing style.

As a kid who knew much more about sidewalks and alleyways than about dusty roads and crop rows, however, this cinematic image—moving though it was—was foreign to me. But when Lightnin's next words came out of the speaker of that record player—"I just can't help but play it on out, just to satisfy myself"—I felt he was speaking for both of us. And those words went straight to my heart. In some ways, the guitar playing seemed more ornate and daunting than anything I was hearing on the other 78s. But after spending countless hours, over many, many months, my fingers started to reproduce on my guitar the notes and timbres that I heard on Lightnin's record. By this time, Lightnin' had become my guitar hero—something that has never changed to this day. And once I began to make my guitar sound like his did, I felt I had found my path through life.

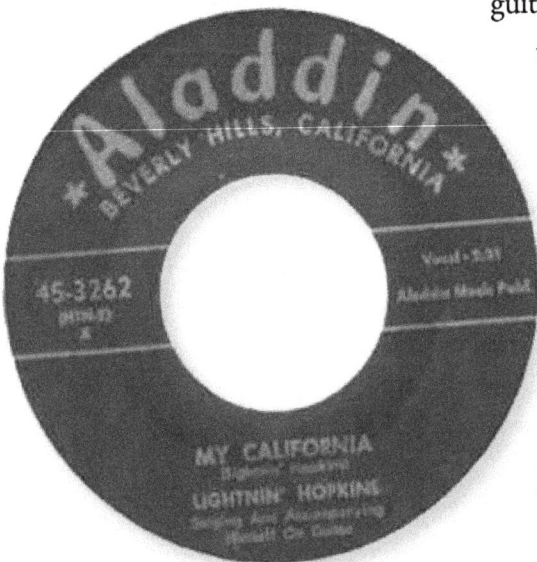

Fast-forward to 1969. By this time, I was playing professionally, and was gigging regularly with blues bands on the South and West Sides of Chicago, including one led by guitar virtuoso Earl Hooker. In May of that year, an agent arranged a tour for Earl's band in California, in order to play a string of dates up and down the coast and record several LPs for ABC-Bluesway. In a last-minute addition to the tour, legendary roots music documentarian Chris Strachwitz used our presence on the West Coast as an opportunity to arrange a session for the band to back up Lightnin' Hopkins for an upcoming Arhoolie Records release.

Needless to say, the thought of recording with one of my all-time heroes was a thrill for me. Here's that California Blues, fer real! A studio in Berkeley was hastily booked, and a few days later we showed up, ready to go to work.

After we recorded a few tracks together, several of us went into the control room, while Lightnin' did a couple of solo tunes. Unbeknownst to the rest of the band, pianist Moose John Walker stayed behind in the main room and was only noticed after the first tune was well in progress. He was sitting on the piano bench and was beginning to slump and doze off during the take. Someone joked "Hope he doesn't snore too loudly" … and sure enough, his snoring became audible through the live mics. We all started laughing but wondered aloud if the taping should continue.

At that point, Lightnin' looked through the control room window, saw us laughing, and looked over his shoulder at Moose—who by now was precariously slumping over and looking like he was about to fall sideways off the bench onto the floor. The tune was a good one up 'til that point, and this most definitely would have ruined the take.

True to form, Lightnin' started channeling the hilarity of the moment into the lyrics he by now was free-associating, which made all of us in the control room laugh twice as loud.

Somehow, Moose managed to remain upright until the end of the tune (a skill acquired during tens of thousands of miles of road touring, no doubt), at which point the recording engineer pressed "stop" on the tape machine, Chris breathed a sigh of relief, the band members broke out in paroxysms of laughter, and Moose was safely whisked away to the control room.

I'm reflecting now about the lifetime of inspiration Lightnin' provided to a 12-year-old kid, whose hair stood on end while listening to a record he found in the back of his dad's record cabinet. I never fail to think about him each year on his birthday. And every other day, for that matter.

Today, as I reminisce about my OWN California Blues experience many years ago, I'm reminded again of my great fortune to have been allowed to "enter that place where the music lived." Somehow, Lightnin's compulsion to "play it on out, just to satisfy myself" has in fact become my own, as well.

I s'pose you COULD say that it's the operating principle of every musician's life and work. I know it's certainly been mine.

Lightnin' Hopkins

Bob Dylan

A Hard Rain and a Stolen Minute

One day in early 1963, when I was 13 years old, my dad asked if I wanted to go with him to a concert of an old music buddy of his, Pete Seeger, at Carnegie Hall.

Sure, why not?

I knew Pete as a family friend—a guy who used to stay at our house when he was in town, like many other of my parents' friends. My parents had been "fellow travelers" with Pete, from labor union concerts of the mid-'40s, through the Henry Wallace presidential campaign and Peoples' Songs days of the late '40s, through the blacklist days of the early-mid '50s. But, truth be told, by 13, my musical passions had already turned to the music of blues and old-time music pickers like Mississippi John Hurt, Lightnin' Hopkins, and Doc Watson. So, I wasn't completely thrilled by the prospect of seeing Pete, with his serviceable banjo strumming and sing-along performing style. But, this was a big concert, in Carnegie Hall … so sure. Why not?

At the end of Pete's first set, he announced that he wanted to introduce the songs of a young songwriter, who was in the house that evening, and whose album had just been released. He proceeded to launch into a song entitled "Who Killed Davey Moore," concerning the death of a boxer who I had never heard of. Coming after Pete's comfortingly familiar favorites, however, this song brought me to full attention, and aroused the pure, passionate outrage that only a 13-year-old can harbor. Pete now had me, as he announced another of this songwriter's songs entitled "A Hard Rain's Gonna Fall."

By now, the hair was standing on the back of my neck—a trick that only Blind Willie Johnson's guitar playing had managed to accomplish until then. But—where the previous song about the boxer gave voice to all my righteous adolescent outrage—THIS song managed to distill every pure expression of what was evil in the world, as well as what was right and beautiful, into a song that felt as old as the hills, or the heavens. Every image of dystopian ugliness, as well as every expression of noble sentiment and heroic impulse, seemed to resonate deep within my thunderstruck 13-year-old soul.

And then, the set was over.

My dad looked at me as the house lights went up, and he could tell I was moved. He said "What did you think?" I must somehow have managed to express my awe, because he said, "Well … should we go backstage and meet the guy who wrote those songs?" I was amazed that he thought we could do that. But of course, Pete was a family friend, my dad was an extroverted kinda guy, and it was actually quite easy.

Minutes later, I was shyly shaking the hand of the guy who wrote the tunes, Bob Dylan, who appeared as uncomfortable with the moment as I was. My dad noticed that there were a few printed copies of a poem on a table nearby that the songwriter had written, and my dad wondered if Bob (we were on a first name basis by then) would sign a copy for me, as a souvenir. He smirked a bit, appearing somewhat ill at ease as he reached for a pen and hastily signed it, cleverly using his printed name as the beginning of his inscription.

A couple of years ago, a friend who's in the art and artifacts business asked me if I still had the autographed copy of the poem. I said, "Yeah, I doubt I would have thrown it out. I must have it somewhere." My friend gently pointed out that I probably should look around for it, as it might be worth something.

I said, "Yeah. You're probably right."

Months passed, and I remembered one day to look for the signed poem. I rummaged around in a couple of boxes where it logically might be, but nothing came of the search. Oh well … maybe it'll turn up eventually.

A couple of years later, I was searching for a photo from a childhood trip to the Ozarks to visit songwriter Jimmy Driftwood (a trip which I describe in greater detail a bit later, in the "Arkansas Traveler" piece). The search meant rummaging around in ANOTHER box, where I had kept photos from tours, travel adventures, and milestones of one sort or another over the decades. And there, at the very bottom of the box, was the signed copy I had been searching for years earlier. Looking at the slightly dog-eared paper, with a coffee stain or two testifying to its owner's careless storage, I was reminded of the name of the poem…"My Life In A Stolen Minute."

I mentioned the discovery to my friend, who asked for a couple of photos. As it turns out, it IS worth something. A LOT of something. All of which seems quite funny to me. But would probably seem even funnier to Bob.

Anyway, all this youthful emotion and memory hit me like a ton of bricks 53 years later, as I watched Patti Smith fight back tears and nerves while performing the song in Stockholm, where Dylan was awarded the 2016 Nobel Prize for Literature.

As she went into the second verse, she stumbled on lyrics she knew well, and then, visibly pained by her mental slip, said, "I'm sorry … can we take that section again? I'm sorry. I'm just so nervous." Her angst at the embarrassing moment was deeply moving, and seems to have touched everyone who viewed the moment on YouTube in the years since.

Smith later said of her performance: "I hadn't forgotten the words that were now a part of me. I was simply unable to draw them out. This strange phenomenon did not diminish or pass but stayed cruelly with me. I was obliged to stop and ask pardon and then attempt again while in this state and sang with all my being, yet still stumbling. It was not lost on me that the narrative of the song begins with the words 'I stumbled alongside of twelve misty mountains,' and ends with the line 'And I'll know my song well before I start singing.' As I took my seat, I felt the humiliating sting of failure, but also the strange realization that I had somehow entered and truly lived the world of the lyrics."

Patti Smith, Stockholm, Sweden

Patti's heartfelt, truly human rendition of the song I first heard so many years ago, sung by Pete at Carnegie Hall, certainly brought it all back home for me.

Was "A Hard Rain's Gonna Fall" Dylan's finest moment as a songwriter? It's certainly not up to me to say. But watching Patti Smith's fully inhabited performance of the song that night, it sure felt like it might have been.

Like Dylan—hell, like EVERYONE at one time or another—I steal a minute or two, and look back on my own life. And looking back at some of those times, it can feel like I too was stumbling up the side of some awfully foggy mountains. And I guess if I were a poet, I too might say that I've walked and I've crawled down some long and winding roads on the journey to where I am today. And dispensing with metaphor, I certainly can acknowledge that I've been more than a little careless with some things that I've picked up along the way, while stumbling up those mountains and down those crooked highways.

Being an artist like Dylan—or like Patti Smith—involves taking a pledge. A pledge that you'll tell it and think it and speak it and breathe it. And then, when provided a stage upon which to do so, reflect it from the mountains so all souls can see it. It's something that, in my own way, I've tried to do myself ever since I decided to devote my life to playing music.

Of course, devoting one's life to something—to ANYTHING—will always be an imperfect pledge. There will always be those mountains to stumble on, and those highways that unanticipatedly veer off into badlands. And those times when you're simply unable to draw out words you know all too well. Or those times when you search fruitlessly for something valuable—something that you carelessly put aside without realizing its importance.

All we can do is the best we can. To take good care of the things that have value. To express the things that need to be said and need to be sung—especially, those things upon which it's impossible to be silent. And hopefully, to know our songs well, before we start singing.

Doc Watson

Fred's Friend That Plays the Git-tar

By the age of 15, I had already assembled a personal pantheon of guitar heroes. At the tippy-top of that heap were Lightnin' Hopkins, Dave Van Ronk, and Mississippi John Hurt. So, imagine my delight when I caught wind of a show in New York City, November 1964, with all three of them. True, it was at Carnegie Hall—not exactly the place one would expect to see a blues show. But still, the opportunity seemed too good to pass up. Especially since I had only HEARD Lightnin' Hopkins on records at that point.

There was another guy on the bill who I'd only heard of by reputation. He was apparently a country guitarist by the name of Doc Watson. (Being an avid Sherlock Holmes fan, I was already intrigued!) I was puzzled by why a country guitarist would appear on the same bill with three blues guitarists—a recollection that now allows me to chuckle at how much a 15-year-old still has to learn.

Anyway, this Watson guy was everything I had imagined him to be, and THEN some. A BIG some. In fact, the amazing renditions of old mountain tunes, gospel hymns, finger style blues, and flat-out bluegrass barnburners, performed by just one guy on guitar was a huge eye-opener for me. For starters, the guy seemed to display an incredible ease, while hitting technical benchmarks that I hadn't known even existed yet. But even more baffling to my youthful perspective was the authority with which this guy performed the entire panorama of American folk music, without ever once appearing false or strained. That ease and authority is a goal that I have striven for in my own playing ever since.

The next spring, my dad was hired to do a magazine article about a guy named Billy Barnes, who worked in Asheville, North Carolina, for one of Lyndon Johnson's War on Poverty programs. My dad asked if I'd like to come along on the trip. On the way down, my dad started dangling hints about a little detour he wanted to take. We turned off the main highway and, as we went farther, the road got rougher and windier, and eventually turned to dirt. At just about the point when I started thinking "Where the hell are we going?" my Dad pointed to a sign and said, "See what that sign says?" I read the sign aloud, which said, "Welcome to Deep Gap."

I said excitedly, "Deep Gap? Dad! Deep Gap is where Doc Watson lives!" My dad said, "It sure is. And we're going to drive up to Doc's house and get him to sign your album!"

Now, mind you … this was early 1965. Doc had only been playing for national audiences for a year or two at this point. So the idea that a couple of strangers would drive up the rutted, muddy road to his front yard unannounced was probably unfamiliar to him, and not entirely welcome. Nevertheless, he and Rosalie made a game attempt to be hospitable to a dad whose son was clearly a fan, albeit a shy one. And after a bit of awkward banter, we got that signature.

I still treasure that original album, with the moody, muted-gray photo on the front, to this day.

Fast forward to 1992, when my then-girlfriend, now-wife Celia and I were driving down to New Orleans for her first taste of the New Orleans Jazz and Heritage Festival. We had more time on our hands back then, so we decided to take slow, "scenic" routes, as opposed to the interstates. While meandering through the back roads of North Carolina, I decided to repeat my dad's mischievous prank. Despite the 27 years, which seemed to have brought some improvement in the road surfaces, the sign reading "Welcome to Deep Gap" was still there.

Now, Celia had served as Box Office Manager for the Flynn Theater for 15 years, so she knew Doc as a performer who consistently sold out the 1,500-seat venue every year or so. I think it's safe to say that Celia was as big a fan of Doc as I was—and for many of the same reasons. Nevertheless, it was with some amusement that she saw the unprepossessing small town that Deep Gap still was in 1992.

On the way out of town, I happened to notice a diner on the left-hand side, with the Blue Plate Special spelled out using those marquee letters one finds throughout the south—whether in front of diners, theaters, or churches. Underneath the lines of type touting the meatloaf, cottage cheese, and wax beans were the words "Appearing Saturday." Underneath that was the letter "D," then a space, and then the letter "C." Underneath that, irregularly spaced, were the letters "W," "T," "O," and "N." I immediately hit the brakes and started to turn around. Celia said in a surprised voice, "WHAT are you doing?"

I said, "Didn't you see that sign?" She said, "You mean about the Blue Plate Special?" I said, "No. Right underNEATH that," and pointed at the sign, which was now directly in front of our car.

She saw the same thing I saw, but apparently wasn't reading it as I was reading it. Because when I said, "Don't you see? It says Doc Watson," she said, "That's ridiculous. First off, it's missing most of the letters. And second off, why in the world would Doc Watson be playing at this tiny diner?" Undeterred by the undeniable logic of her points, I said, "I'm going to go in and ask."

Since by now it was well past lunchtime, there were only a few regulars still sitting at the counter. I had to wait a bit before I could get the attention of the waitress, who obviously had better things to do then to wait on the stranger who had just walked in. Upon capturing her indifferent attention, I said, "Sorry to bother you, ma'am. But could you tell me what the sign outside says, underneath the Blue Plate Special?" Her vacant look made it clear that she had no idea what I was talking about, and not much interest in finding out. I decided to take the plunge into the water of my harebrained theory and asked, "Is there someone who plays here on Saturday nights?"

Without any change in her bored expression, she said, "Oh honey, there's just some fella who's a friend of the owner, who plays here sometime." Seeing my expression

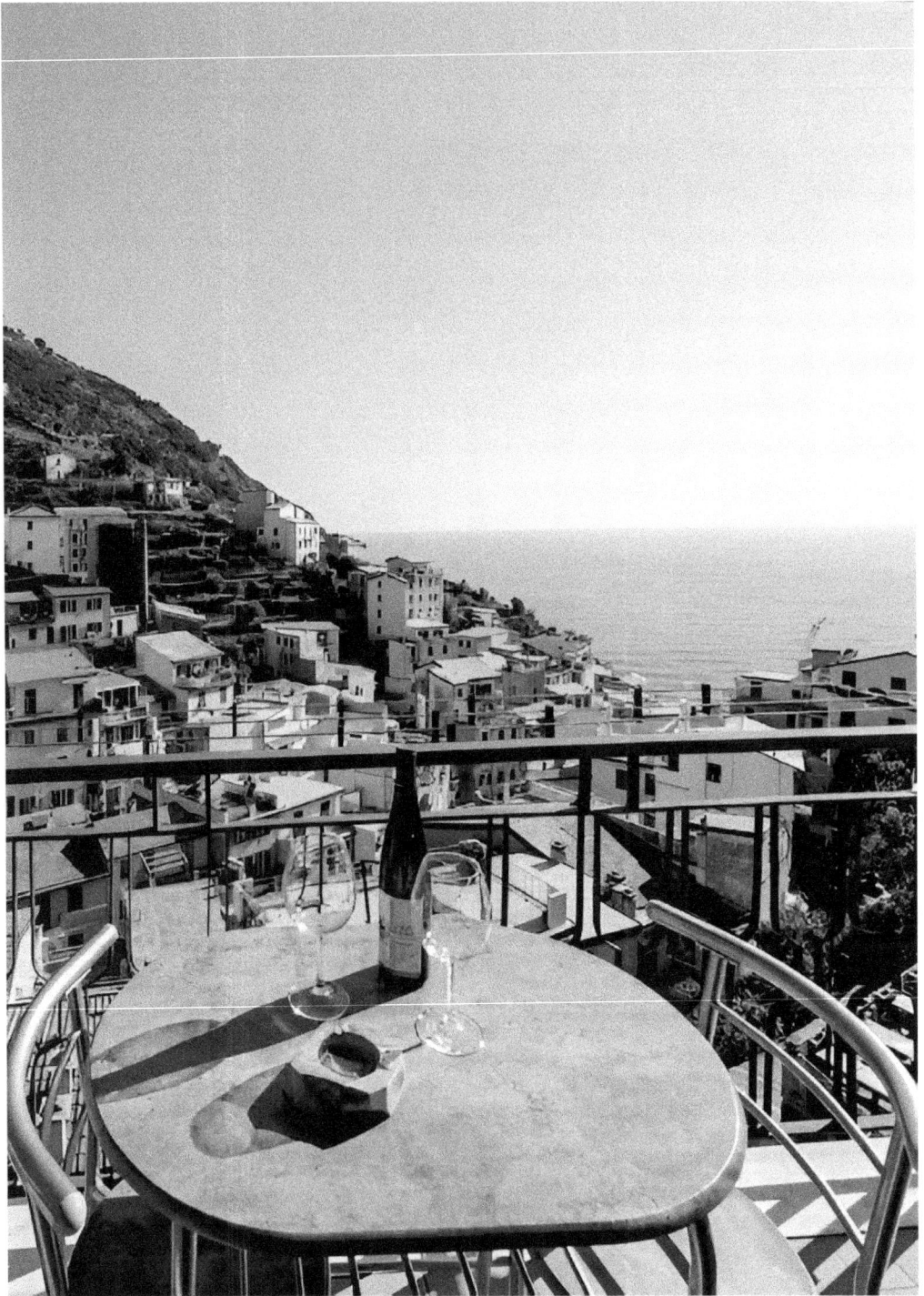

of interest, she pointed to a far corner of the room, where there were some boxes of canned goods and soda, and said, "Yeah, he sets up over there and sings and plays the git-tar." I said "Is his name Doc Watson?" As an expression somewhere between irritation and amusement flickered across her face, she turned to the kitchen and yelled "Hey, Sam! What's the name of that boy that plays in the corner on Saturday night? You know…Fred's friend, who plays the git-tar?"

Sam yelled back something that was apparently as incomprehensible to her as it was to me. She looked at me with an expression that contained a bit more irritation and a bit less amusement then earlier and said, "What did you say his name was again?" I said, "Doc. Doc Watson." She turned again to the kitchen and yelled, "Is his name Watson, or something like that?" This time, Sam's reply was a bit clearer.

"Yeah. That sounds about right."

So, there you have it. A man can travel across the globe—touching literally millions of people with his charmingly unadorned personality, setting impossibly high standards for those guitarists unfortunate enough to follow in his wake, and inspiring thousands of musicians to think a bit broader about how to play and present their music—and still be a stranger in his own small hometown. Life's funny that way.

Fast forward again, to 2012. Celia and I were in Italy, at a festival dedicated to American "Roots Music"—a term that would've puzzled Doc, no doubt, but a category which he is as responsible for as anyone in the history of American music. I was sitting on the balcony of our *pensione*, catching a bit of Wi-Fi from the café across the street, when I read the news that Doc had passed. Writing this, years later, I still get choked up by the memory, and of American music's collective loss.

Doc just turned 100 last year. I almost began that last sentence by saying, "If Doc was still here … " But of course, Doc IS still here. And he always WILL be here, wherever American music itself is listened to, played, and celebrated.

Happy 100th birthday, Doc. There'll never be another like you.

Sam Lay and Those Gold Shoes

By 1965, I was beginning to dally a bit in my romance with the Martin 00-18 acoustic guitar that my dad had bought me for my 13th birthday. A dalliance you might call "Hiking the Appalachian Trail"…except, with an electric guitar, instead of a woman in Buenos Aires.

I know what you're thinking. It was the Beatles on *The Ed Sullivan Show* that did it, right? Well, not exactly.

Don't get me wrong. Like practically every teenager, I was intrigued by the Fab Four's prelude to world domination on that night in '64. But no…unlike many of my musical peers, it wasn't those long-haired moptops that prompted my trail hike into the electric world.

It was a pair of records that I bought the very next year—the first being "Hoodoo Man Blues" by Junior Wells, followed soon after by the debut album of "The Paul Butterfield Blues Band," that lured me to the dark side. The slinkiness of that first record, and the fire and drive of the second, proved to be a collective siren song that won me over, where the Fab Four had failed.

The cool-looking cover of the Butterfield album showed five bad-looking dudes leaning against a funky wall of a notions shop on Maxwell Street. The window of the shop advertised its wares—incense, herbs, oils, and similar Voodoo-related paraphernalia—all of which would be quite familiar to the Mississippi and Louisiana-born residents of the South Side of Chicago, where I lived. But at that time, in 1965, the typical American record-buying teenager was used to seeing quite different images on

the covers of their record albums—and quite different fashion notions purveyed by the artists—than these five rough-looking customers standing in front of a Voodoo shop were projecting.

For perspective, try and imagine how exotic that same photo background must have appeared to fans of the Beatles, or of British blues-rock groups like the Yardbirds and the Rolling Stones—groups who dressed in trendy, faux-Victorian "mod" stage clothes and presented as androgynous, long-haired "pretty boys" in their publicity photos and album covers. By contrast, the blues artists whose music the English bands were emulating wore business suits while performing, and doo-rags and undershirts when off-stage.

Though looking nothing like musicians in Chicago blues bands, these British blues-rock groups were nevertheless on a passionate mission to alert America to the music that had been birthed in its Black communities in the early 1900s—and had continued to evolve and thrive there, unbeknownst to white listeners, for many decades after.

It's an oft-repeated fact that many music fans—both in England and in the U.S.—first heard American R&B tunes from the Stones' versions, which filled their first few albums. But less-mentioned in the music press is how many of those same music fans would eventually hail Paul Butterfield's first album as their gateway drug into a harder-edged music, which ultimately would have an even greater impact on the pop and rock world—electric Chicago blues.

Having grown up on the South Side of Chicago myself, I didn't find the cover of that Butterfield album especially exotic. In fact, to me, the setting and the way the members were dressed looked quite familiar—which perhaps is why I was initially drawn to the Butterfield album while most of my friends were listening to the Beatles, the Kinks, and the Stones. But whatever the reason, I spent a lot of time staring at that funky album jacket and its Maxwell Street photo. As one did back in the days of 12-inch LPs, long before anyone referred to them as "vinyl."

However, there was one thing that I was never clear on, and that none of my friends seemed to know the answer to, either. Which one of these guys was ACTUALLY Paul Butterfield, the namesake band leader?

The guy that initially struck me as the toughest-looking of these five dudes was the big guy in the middle wearing an undershirt and those wild gold shoes. I initially assumed that he was the bandleader, Paul Butterfield. But no, Paul turned out to be the guy to his right, wearing a rumpled, nondescript, brown corduroy jacket. As I soon learned, that tough-looking guy with the gold shoes was the drummer—and that drummer's name was Sam Lay.

Before working in Butter's band, Sam had held down the drum chair in Howlin' Wolf's terrific band for years and was known around Chicago as one of the strongest, groovin'-est drummers on the scene. Since Wolf worked constantly, Sam was one of the WORKIN'-est guys on the scene as well—which meant Butter must've made Sam an awfully good offer to leave Wolf.

History quickly proved that Butter's offer was a smart choice for Sam. Within a year or two, the Butterfield Band was not only the hottest thing in Chicago but quickly became a major coast-to-coast touring act. East Coast and West Coast audiences quickly discovered what Chicago audiences knew for years—when old-school blues goes electric, the increased volume brings with it increased fire and rhythmic punch.

The fire may have come from guitarist Mike Bloomfield, whose virtuosic playing inspired several generations of electric players from Carlos Santana to Eddie Van Halen. But that rhythmic punch was largely thanks to one man—Sam Lay.

And then…Bob Dylan happened. The '65 Newport Folk Festival was a breakout moment for Sam, for electric blues, and for the electrification of folk music. Tours and recordings with Dylan, James Cotton, The Chambers Brothers, and others followed. But then, Sam contracted pleurisy, and had to take time off the road to recuperate. By the time Sam finally recovered, the Butterfield Band had hired a new drummer, Billy Davenport, to replace him.

By 1968, Sam had recovered his health and started working on a vision for his own band. I received a call, along with my bandmate Jeff Carp, to be part of that vision—an offer we both jumped at eagerly. Sam's previous bandmates included veteran guitarists Louis Myers and Hubert Sumlin and harmonica titan Little Walter, and these were the men whose big shoes Sam wanted us to fill. It's hard to imagine a more valuable apprenticeship than the daunting assignment Sam signed me and Jeff up for!

Working with Sam was a trip. And the trippiest part was how incredibly different Sam was from the initial impression I got when staring at that Butterfield Band cover. Sam was a pussycat, with his heart charmingly worn on his sleeve 24 hours a day. In place of the street-tough cussing that I had imagined, there was "Dagnabbit," "Yee Doggie," and hilarious malapropisms and mispronunciations. No "straight outta Compton" for Sam. It was more like "straight outta Beverly Hillbillies." And though considerably older and far more experienced than we were, Sam's idealism and childlike enthusiasm for the music was at least as strong as mine and Jeff's was.

Sam could be childlike in other ways, too. Like, how he got 10 different colors of shoes.

By the time Sam decided to front his own band, he had gotten well-known for those gold shoes on the album cover. So, Sam came up with a brilliant idea.

He found a mail-order place that specialized in outfitting entire bands with shoes. But actually, Sam wasn't interested in outfitting the whole band with shoes. He was just looking for a bunch of shoes for HIM. So, he figured out a clever ruse.

The company offered 10 different colors of shoes. So, Sam told the company that he had a 10-piece band, and he wanted everyone to be wearing different colors. Oh… and one more thing. He told them every member of the band wore size 12EE.

And THAT'S how he got 10 different colors of shoes.

There are MANY other stories—some of which I'd be struggling to find a family-friendly way to relate. One of them that IS family-friendly involves a recording session we did in (I think) 1968.

Sam was told by an agent that he needed a recording of the band in order to get more gigs beyond Chicago and Detroit, where most of our gigs were. So Sam arranged a session. But at the last minute, he threw everyone a curveball. He decided that in order to allow him to concentrate on his singing, he needed to hire his Butterfield Band replacement, Billy Davenport, to play drums instead of him.

WHAAT? None of us in the band thought it was a good idea, as Sam was clearly the better man for the job. But Sam was the leader, obviously. So that settled that. Billy did a good job, but the session definitely would have swung harder if Sam had played instead.

Oh, well. What can ya do? Chalk it up as just another unfortunate decision, made in the heat of the moment, that wound up as a footnote in the imperfect legacy of yet another journeyman Chicago bluesman.

I last saw Sam when my wife and I visited Chicago for a record-breaking, bone-chillingly cold week in January '96. Sam was playing in a small club on the North Side, and on the break, I went up to greet Sam and invite him over to our table. The look on Sam's face was absolutely priceless and will remain with me forever.

After several minutes of catching up on old and new times, Sam cut to the chase. "Hey, man. When are you gonna move back to Chicago? I need you here, man. I've never had a band that sounded as good as the one that you and Jeff were in with me." I said jokingly, "Oh, Sam… I'll bet you say that to ALL the girls." And then, the smile on Sam's face vanished.

"No, man. I'm serious. None of these guys can play the shit right, the way you guys did. I MEAN it, dagnabbit! Please tell me you'll move back here and play with me."

I still think that Sam's words that night were attributable to his being swept up in heartfelt emotion, heightened by not having seen one another for many decades. (I TOLD you he was a pussycat!) And I hope I'm right about that, because it makes me sad to think that he felt let down by the players he'd had in recent years, after playing with Wolf, Muddy, Walter, Cotton, Butterfield, and the other greats of the '60s.

But that said, I'd be lying if I pretended I wasn't flattered to hear those words from one of my most valued early mentors.

Sam passed away in January 2022, at the age of 87. But Yee Doggie… you were one-of-a-kind, Sam. They truly broke the mold after you came along.

Sam Lay in the '50s

I'll never forget how lucky I was to spend those years on stage with you, and how much you taught a young 19-year-old kid.

"Sky Songs" From Booker

In the fall of 1967, I began my second year of classes at University of Chicago, and (as mentioned earlier, in "Rich Men, and a Rich Man's Woman") I moved into a dingy apartment with two friends from freshman year. A few months later, over Christmas break at term's end, I hitchhiked to Mexico, with a fuzzy, hastily arranged plan to meet one of my roommates in Mexico City.

To get there, I took a second-class train, which turned out to be filled with Mexican farm families and their livestock. The train car was unheated and got freezing cold at night, making it almost impossible to sleep. Nevertheless, I must have dozed off at some point—because when I awoke, I discovered I no longer had my wallet, which contained not only all my IDs, but also all the cash my parents had allotted towards my living expenses for Spring term.

Upon realizing that I now had almost no money, and no proof of US citizenship, I felt a brief moment of panic. However, the panic quickly subsided … and in its wake, I was left with an odd feeling of release. A decision seemed called for, and my sleep-deprived brain lunged in the direction of the first one that bubbled up and presented itself to my now fully conscious mind. That decision-bubble quickly gelled into a plan—upon returning home to Chicago, I would quit school, and hopefully get enough gigs in the blues clubs I had been frequenting to pay my third of the rent and keep myself fed.

Admittedly, the decision was a crazy one, one that only a 19-year-old kid could persuade himself made any sense whatsoever. Nevertheless, by February 1968, the plan was in full effect.

Backstage after the Friday night concert of the eighth annual folk festival of the University of Chicago. Bukka White still held his audience entranced playing the blues. Listening left to right are Paul Asbell, 5240 Kenwood, Ralph Kogan, 1030 E. 49th, White, Herman Sinaiko, 5123 Greenwood, and Allister Crowley from the University of Wisconsin.

One afternoon, I received a phone call from a grad student friend named Mark Greenberg, who I knew from his work coordinating the UC Folk Festival. One of the performers the festival was planning to bring in was a Mississippi bluesman named Bukka White. Did I know the name?

Well, I most certainly DID know the name. In fact, his song "Fixin' To Die" was one of the ones that had utterly transfixed me when I heard it on a Sam Charters-produced album of old 78 recordings called *The Country Blues*, which I had bought five years earlier. Well, OK. So, would I be willing to put him up for a few days, while he was in town performing? Of course, I would. And since one of my roommates regularly stayed at his girlfriend's house anyway, there was a bed free for Bukka.

A brief digression at this point. I knew the man's name as Bukka—because, after all, Bukka was the name that appeared on the LP I owned. And, Bukka was the name that appeared on the label of the original 78 recording he made in 1940. And Bukka was the name he was called at the UC Folk Festival. And for that matter, the name that appeared on the marquee of coffeehouses and folk festivals all over the country since his "rediscovery" in 1963.

But, Bukka WASN'T ACTUALLY HIS NAME. I mean … have you EVER heard the name "Bukka" before, or since? Of course not. Because the man's name was Booker Washington White—and somehow, neither John Lomax nor Lester Melrose nor any of the folks who had recorded him and released his records over three decades ever realized that fact. Or thought to make the correction. Booker himself realized the mistake, of course. When asked about the misspelling many years later, he said, "I liked one of them Ks, but not the other."

But getting back to the man's visit …

To be honest, I don't remember a whole lot of anecdotes about the time Booker spent in our apartment, or about the answers to the many questions I'm sure I must have pestered my guest with. What I DO remember, however, is the amazing full-throated roar that emerged from Booker's National steel guitar when he performed his tunes.

Do you remember the Maxell ad from the early '80s, with the guy sitting in his chair in front of his hi-fi speaker, with his hair peeled back from the force of the sound? Well, that was what it was

NO OTHER AUDIO TAPE DELIVERS HIGHER FIDELITY.

like, sitting six feet away from Booker White, as he played "Aberdeen"—and many other songs that he was fond of saying he extemporaneously plucked from the sky—while sitting in a straight-back chair in my living room.

The word "powerful" doesn't begin to convey the experience.

A few years ago, a friend discovered the picture on the facing page in the UC newspaper, *The Maroon*. Looking at a young version of me, along with a number of UC dignitaries and other performers on the show, instantly brought back the memory of the time when "sky-song-creator," cousin to B.B. King and seminal Mississippi bluesman Booker Washington White came to stay.

Wayne Bennett

"Up, Up, and Away"— My Lesson with Wayne Bennett

One day in the spring of 1968, I learned that an iconic guitarist named Wayne Bennett—a man whom I had revered and listened to for years—lived just a few blocks away in my neighborhood. I was 19, already gigging in blues clubs, and knew a fair amount about my neighbor's storied career—playing with nationally-known acts like Bobby Blue Bland, Little Junior Parker, and the entire Duke Records stable of artists, as well as locally with Jesse Jackson's Operation Breadbasket band and other high-profile performers. I had seen Wayne several times at the corner drugstore and finally worked up the nerve to ask him if he would give me a lesson. He looked me over for a few seconds and, based on that preliminary inspection, said "Sure. That'd be fine." He then gave me his address and told me a time a few days from then when I should come by.

On the appointed day, I walked the few blocks to Wayne's house. After exchanging a few pleasantries, he had me sit down with my Gibson ES-295 and said to me, "What would you like to learn?" I described why I had come. I told him I hoped he could show me some more stuff about how to broaden my blues playing—how to be more sophisticated and literate, like HIS playing was.

Wayne said, "Well, let's play a little bit together." Which we did. After a few choruses, at the point when it was just starting to feel good, Wayne stopped, waved his hand, and said, "Okay. Fine. You can play the blues pretty well." Which, of course, I was delighted to hear. Then he said, "So we're not gonna work on that."

Sensing my disappointment, Wayne said, "Look. You can already DO that. If you want to make a living as a professional, you're going to have to know how to play a heckuva lot more than just blues."

I started to point out that I already was somewhat versed in some other styles, but Wayne quickly blew past that and said, "We're going to work on the kind of tunes you'll need to know if you want to be a truly well-rounded musician." And with that, he started to play a song that I recognized from the radio at a local grocery store. The song was by a group called the 5th Dimension, called "Up, Up and Away."

This was DEFINITELY not what I pictured was going to happen in my lesson with the great Wayne Bennett. However, I gamely struggled through it ... and at some point, Wayne presumably realized he had created as much disturbance in the mind of a young 19-year-old as the afternoon warranted. He said, "Well, keep working on it, and when you get it, come back and we'll work on some more tunes." I thanked him, asked what I owed, paid the small sum he asked for, and sheepishly waved goodbye as I made my way down the stairs to the street.

I never returned for another lesson.

But Wayne's message about expanding one's musical horizons became increasingly clear over the months that followed. And proved to be an indispensable godsend two years later, when I was tasked with following in veteran guitarist Matt Murphy's footsteps in a trio that played all sorts of music besides the blues styles that Wayne had been so insistent I would need to set aside. (My tribute to Matt can be found in a subsequent chapter on page 54.)

As a teacher of over 55 years now, I have to say that I don't approach similar situations with my students in the same way that Wayne did with me. I've come to believe that the teacher needs to meet the student where they're presently at NOW. And then, use the music the student is currently in love with to build a bridge into the new territory that lies further on up the road.

But musicians of Wayne's generation came up in a school chock-full of hard knocks that mirrored the pre-Dr. Spock parenting approach found all over the rural south. In that school, "time-outs" were something that happened on the football field rather than in the home, and whuppings were an essential part of the curriculum. When measured by the standard of how Wayne and most of his peers were raised, the message I was given was an awfully gentle one.

Looking back on it now, 56 years later, it's clear to me that my lesson with Wayne certainly provided the timely wake-up call of real-world information that this particular northern-bred 19-year-old needed. Even if he didn't think so at the time.

More recently, I went to see the fantastic film *Summer of Soul*, which prominently featured so many of my favorite artists from the late '60s. (In the extremely unlikely event that anyone with tastes like mine HASN'T seen it—rectify that situation at once. It's an absolute "must-see!")

Upon reading the list of performers that made the cut in the released version of the film—and seeing Jesse Jackson's Operation Breadbasket Band featured—I peeled my eyes to see if Wayne was in there. But as it turned out, the eye-peeling wasn't necessary. Wayne played a highly visible, highly audible role in the deeply soulful presentation of "Precious Lord" with Mavis Staples and Mahalia Jackson. What a delightfully unexpected surprise!

Hardly a day goes by that I don't listen to or think about Wayne. For starters, his playing on Bobby "Blue" Bland's incredibly deep oeuvre represents a "must-hear" soundtrack for anyone aspiring to be a blues guitarist. Hell … his solo on "Stormy Monday Blues" is one of the sacred texts of our entire canon. I never tire of marveling at the perfection of it.

Wayne was born on December 13, 1932. He passed away in 1992, at the age of 59. It's a true privilege to offer a shoutout to one of the finest guitarists in blues and R&B history, Wayne Bennett.

Earl Hooker

Guitar Heroes

In 1968, I got hired to play rhythm guitar for a guy who had been a hero of mine for several years—a Chicago-based blues guitarist named Earl Hooker. By that time, I had already gotten turned on to jazz players like George Benson, as well as to fellow South Side players like George Freeman, Wayne Bennett, and Reggie Boyd. But I hadn't quite grasped how to combine those guys' jazz styles with the more explosive, biting sound of the electric players who I loved and had been emulating—guys like Buddy Guy and Otis Rush. As skilled as these jazz guys were, I never heard any of 'em play singing slide melodies like Robert Nighthawk, lead guitar breaks like B.B. King and Otis Rush, or Chicago-style blues backup like Louis Myers and Robert Jr. Lockwood.

Earl did all those things on a nightly basis, as well as effortlessly fitting in bebop-inflected solos on blues standards, or tossing off country licks like Texas Troubadour Buddy Charleton when the situation called for it.

That versatility undoubtedly came from the need to please audiences of different complexions and different musical tastes, as Earl traveled all over the South and the Midwest. His enthusiasm for getting the details of each style so "right" showed me what a restless imagination—combined with tens of thousands of nights of gigs—could accomplish.

It didn't take me long to understand why every musician I met while working with Earl referred to him in hushed tones of reverence. Even B.B. King was known to say that his favorite blues guitarist was Earl Hooker—and that he wouldn't be caught dead taking the stand and playing after Earl had got done burning it down.

Working with Earl Hooker night after night on the bandstand certainly served as a powerful motivator for me at age 20, and continues to inspire my own playing to this

day. Like so many players, however, Earl exemplified the term "musician's musician" and never became as well-known to the general public as he was to his peers. Whether because of his less-than-powerful voice, weakened by tuberculosis in later years, or his less-than-Hollywood looks, the glowing praise and admiration Earl received from B.B., Buddy Guy, Jimi Hendrix. and many others never resulted in the "household name" status that those iconic performers enjoyed.

Which is why I was surprised to receive a letter while on tour with Paul Butterfield from a French author named Sebastian Danchin, asking if I might be willing to grant him an interview on Earl's career, life and legacy. Which of COURSE I was delighted to do! Sebastian was able to similarly interview scores of other fellow musicians and music business professionals who worked with Earl, and the resulting book, *Earl Hooker: Blues Master*, provides both a detailed timeline of Earl's career and the fascinating, often hilarious stories of his life and times. I highly recommend it to anyone who'd like to know more about a fine musician who's flown below the radar of so many fans of Chicago blues.

Around 20 years ago, I was swapping stories about old times spent on the South Side scene in the '60s with my old buddy Dick Shurman. Over the last 50 years, Dick has parlayed his fascination and encyclopedic knowledge of blues lore into a long, award-filled career producing albums and writing liner notes and magazine articles for major blues publications. Dick's seemingly photographic memory for details—everything from discography particulars to addresses of clubs to historical specifics of the men I once called my employers—has been an inestimable blessing in reminding me of episodes and escapades whose details time had all but washed away.

Otis Rush

During our enjoyable hang, Dick related an anecdote to me that I had never heard before, of an afternoon spent at Otis Rush's place, listening to the 1969 "Don't Have to Worry" recording Earl's band had done on ABC BluesWay. (More on this recording can be found in my story entitled "I'll Just Sit Here And Do What I Do.") According to Dick, a solo came up (which can be heard at 2:24 on the title track "Don't Have to Worry") and Otis excitedly said, "Yeah, now THERE'S the Earl Hooker that I wanna hear!"

Dick then said to me, "But Paul—that was YOUR solo!"

When Dick told me that, I choked up … for reasons I've thought a lot about, but am still trying to fully wrap my head around. I think the reason for my emotion was because—for me—Otis's apparent mis-attribution was the greatest compliment I could ever imagine receiving.

You see, like Earl, Otis was someone who was a hero and a huge inspiration for me, as he was for so many other players. But despite the accolades and respect that he received from his fellow musicians, Otis was a man who had a hard time believing in his own self-worth. I remember a time when Otis was driving me home from a gig we had played at Peppers, and I complimented him on how he sounded that night. Otis shook his head, indicating how little pleasure he took in my compliment. He said, "Paul, if I could just play like Kenny Burrell and sing like Wilson Pickett, I'd be happy."

No amount of protestations to the contrary could make him accept how great he was, or how much he was admired.

I was deeply touched by Dick's story: that is, when Otis heard the stylistic stuff that I had copped from HIM—and then heard that same stuff on Earl's recording, but played by ME—he loved it. But I can't help but wonder if it would have moved him as much if he had heard the same licks and phrasing being played by him on his OWN recording.

I firmly believe that the REASON he loved it as much as he apparently did was because he thought it was HIS hero, Earl Hooker, playing it.

The phrase "rock star" is everywhere nowadays. It's used to describe exceptional high-school athletic coaches, up-and-coming middle-management corporate hires, chefs at au courant restaurants, PTA teachers of the year, and other outstanding individuals whose skills and accomplishments within their profession led to them being placed on a pedestal by their peers. The fact that most of these folks would look a bit ridiculous posing lasciviously with a pointy-headed electric guitar strapped on at thigh level is part of the ironic charm of the term, I s'pose.

It's worth noting, however, that nobody in the blues world refers to outstanding players within the genre as "rock stars." After all, the term evokes images of youthful appeal and adolescent concerns—and blues is not, and has never really been, music intended to appeal to young people.

But as anyone who looks at music magazines and record albums can plainly see, the blues world DOES have "guitar heroes." And as the packaging of the eponymously named video game reminds us, the term "guitar hero" can similarly be understood as evoking those same images of youth and adolescent concerns. In other words, strictly kids' stuff—with the implied understanding that once someone grows up, they inevitably take their heroes off the pedestal they once were placed on.

My experience with the older players that I learned my craft from, however, suggests a different understanding. Almost invariably, the men I knew and worked under had heroes themselves—heroes whose luster didn't seem to tarnish in their eyes as the years went by. For Otis Rush and B.B., it was Earl Hooker. For Buddy Guy, it was Guitar Slim and Muddy Waters. And on and on it goes …

I see the same thing in myself, as I write these words. The men who I admired, and passionately put on a pedestal as a kid, are still my heroes to this day. Earl and Otis—you're right up there now, on that same pedestal I put you on sixty years ago.

And, I expect, you always will be.

Matt Murphy

Matt "Guitar" Murphy

In the early months of 1970, after freelancing in South Side Chicago blues clubs for several years, my drummer friend Kennard Johnson gave me a tip on the down-low concerning a band he was playing with 6 nights a week, whose regular guitarist would soon be moving onto a national, hi-profile gig. The band was called "King Tut and the Carburetors," and they played some blues, a lot of current R&B, and some jazz tunes as well, when called for. The pay was good, compared with what I had gotten used to, but the hours were 10PM to 4AM and 10PM to 5AM on Saturday nights.

Long, long hours. Was I interested?

Along with my bassist friend Clyde Stats, I drove out to the club, to check Kennard and the band out.

The band was just a trio, with Tut simultaneously playing complex bass lines and singing like Stevie Wonder, and Kennard playing powerful drums. Without a keyboardist, the guitarist had a big job. His name was Matt "Guitar" Murphy, and listening to a couple of sets with the band was enough to let me know that if Matt were indeed to leave, I would have VERY big shoes to fill.

I knew Matt by reputation because he had already had a long career playing with Memphis Slim, Howlin' Wolf, Junior Parker, Ike Turner, Bobby Blue Bland, Muddy Waters, and many others, and his name was well-known to the small group of musicians who were passionate about blues lore in those days. Along with his brother Floyd, Matt was responsible for creating the signature guitar licks and musical hooks for many tunes which are now considered blues standards; tunes which are routinely played in bars across the country to this day, and enjoyed by audiences who've likely never heard Matt Murphy's name.

However, here Matt was, in Carol's Lounge, not only playing blues, but also current pop material, jazz standards, an occasional country tune, and virtually everything else that the gig required over five to six hours of music per night. The fact that Matt handled it all with aplomb, facility, and zest—evidencing no apparent preference for any one of the styles more than another—wound up making a huge impression on me. One that would last a lifetime.

Well, Matt wound up taking the gig a few weeks later and left Chicago for good. Matt's new gig was as a featured member of his longtime music partner James Cotton's band, and lasted for many years, until he found newfound fame—if not fortune—from a featured role in *The Blues Brothers* movies and subsequent touring.

Once Matt left, the gig was mine, and I stayed in it for a year or so, until I had saved enough money so that my girlfriend and I could make a long-dreamed-of move to rural Vermont, to begin a new life. But that's a whole 'nother story, which I'll cover a bit later in this book.

Matt's incredibly long, illustrious career as sideman to virtually every major artist in the blues world puts him in rarified company, for people like me. If the music industry gave out "Best Supporting Actor" awards to players, Matt would have scored many of 'em, as well as receiving a "Lifetime Achievement Award" for his remarkable contributions to the blues.

But equally admirable to me, and to his fellow musicians, was Matt's neverending pride in his thorough musicianship, in the excellent physical shape he kept himself in while traveling on the road, and in his deep relationships with his family and his fellow man.

Matt was born in Sunflower, Mississippi on December 29, 1929. He passed away in 2018, at the age of 89.

RIP, monster guitarist Matt "Guitar" Murphy.

Duxbury, Vermont 1971

Beyond Category

In 1971, after my brief lifetime immersed in a professional music career in Chicago, I was casting about for a change—presumably, another busy music scene to wade into. My then-girlfriend had just finished college and also felt ready to make a fresh start somewhere else—presumably, a university with a strong graduate program. However, the "back to the land" movement was in full swing, and it had swept up many of our friends in its powerful, heady wake. Ignoring the logic of career arcs and academic pursuance, we opted for a dramatic lifestyle change without any clear view of what lay ahead.

We bought land halfway up a steep mountain road in northern Vermont—and there, with a small amount of savings from my six night/week gig in Chicago, armed with the *Whole Earth Catalog* and some borrowed tools, we built a geodesic dome in which to start our new life.

For a couple of years, we lived "off the grid"—at first, quite literally, with no electric power. But, even after we eventually hooked up the juice, we remained quite disconnected from popular culture of any sort for several years. (To this day, when a pop song or movie reference is unfamiliar to me, I ask, "Was that between 1971 and '73?")

Around 1974, shortly after plugging back in, my girlfriend developed a strong infatuation with a record called *Pretzel Logic* by a group calling itself Steely Dan. I recognized instantly the William Burroughs-inspired band name and was further intrigued by the obvious Dylan reference in the album she acquired shortly afterwards, *Can't Buy A Thrill*. These were smart guys, and I grudgingly admitted that the songwriting was indeed awfully clever. But I was quite a creature of musical habit in those days—and still am, I suppose—and the music clearly struck me as "white rock." SMART white rock, to be sure, but seemingly not beholden to the instrumental textures or vocal conventions of Black R&B in any way. As a result, I just couldn't dig it. (My girlfriend was certainly more prescient than I was on that score.)

Things started to change a bit with "Katy Lied" and "The Royal Scam," but it wasn't until "Aja" in 1977 that I fell head-over-heels in love, and thoroughly onboard. Had the rhythm section playing—clearly closer now to R&B than to rock—actually become more slinky, funky, and sensuous? Or was it that I just never noticed how good it was before? Were the harmonic underpinnings—obviously inspired by Duke Ellington and Wayne Shorter and other jazz heroes of mine—much more ambitiously and fully realized now? Or was it that I just missed it in the earlier tunes because the timbres were closer to rock than jazz?

Hard to say.

All I know is that by then, I too was writing music underpinned by funk and R&B rhythms—but with harmonic and melodic ideas more beholden to jazz than pop music—and Steely Dan had clearly staked out similar turf, with artistic and commercial success beyond what anyone could have predicted. Their success was an exhilarating, encouraging sign for groups like the one I formed in 1977 (which performed under the name "The Paul Asbell Quartet" for a year or so before being renamed Kilimanjaro). But at the same time, the visionary arrangements, instrumental and vocal track production values, and unprecedented sonic excellence set a terrifyingly high benchmark for anyone bold enough to compete on similar turf.

THIS I could dig. And did.

Among my music friends, the widely divergent opinions concerning Steely Dan's music seem to fall into distinct categories. There are the music nerds, who appreciate the ambition, complexity, and innovation of the music—lyrically, instrumentally, and compositionally. Then, there are the hit radio fans, who were initially sucked in by the incredibly well-crafted rhythm tracks and eventually grew to love them as pop anthems. But then again, there are those who hate the music, seeing it as annoyingly meticulous, formulaic pop artifice. (I find myself wondering what "formula" they're thinking of … but that's another tangent for another time).

But whatever one thinks of the work, these two guys raised the bar of sheer ambition in pop music to a dizzyingly high level, putting them in the category of the Beatles and precious few others. And, like the Beatles, Becker and Fagen eventually decided

Steely Dan in the '70s

that their studio creations could not be successfully rendered live and stopped performing as a band in '74. They did very little touring for 30 years afterwards, and even after that, little in the US.

In 2014, I noticed that the group was playing dates in the Northeast with my Chicago homie, Bobby Broom, opening the show. One afternoon in August, at 4:20, Celia and I were discussing what we should do for dinner, when I jokingly pointed out that Bobby and the Dan were both performing at 7:30 that evening in Gilford, New Hampshire. Gilford is just under three hours away … so if we left right that minute, we could just make it in time to catch the show.

Suffice it to say, Celia was game.

By 4:40, we had bought tix and a parking pass, printed them out, jumped in the car, and drove like a banshee to Gilford. We got there just as Bobby was starting his set, which was a predictably fine one. Steely Dan, of course, sounded fantastic. Their deeply ambitious music was made all the more so by rearrangements that featured each band member, much as Ellington did. The arrangements didn't always feel congruent with the iconic arrangements we've heard for decades—but huge props to Fagen and Becker for going for it in true, re-inventive jazz tradition.

Sadly, guitarist/lyricist and acerbic wit Walter Becker passed in 2017. But that hasn't stopped the Dan from touring and continuing to raise the bar for what we all can expect from a "pop music" performance.

In 2013, I released my third solo CD, From *Adamant To Atchafalaya*. On it, I included my version of one of my favorite Dan tunes, "Deacon Blues." The song's lyrics are a bittersweet ode to a darkly romanticized jazzman's life, as viewed through the eyes of an alternate-identity-seeking suburban kid. In Becker's lyrics, the kid rejects the cultural supremacy of the named winners of the world, seeking instead for a name when he loses.

In the world of skilled, audacious, and ground-breaking harmonica playing, there IS in fact a name for the winner—

Steely Dan in 2007

and that name is Howard Levy. I knew when Howard offered to play on the tune with me that it would be pure magic. Do me a favor and listen to it—and tell me if you don't agree!

Duke Ellington had a phrase he used to bestow the very highest compliment possible on a musical artist. He would say they were "beyond category." In my opinion, if anyone in the realm of pop music fits that description, it's Steely Dan.

Clouds of Hashish Smoke ... From Both Sides Now

Around 5:30 one morning in early 1968, my girlfriend and I were awakened from a sound sleep by a loud, insistent knock on the apartment's front door, followed by a voice bellowing, "Open up!"

Living where we did, one always felt a certain level of anxiety about what dangers might await in the streets outside our door. Petty burglars, late-night drunks, enraged street people, traumatized Vietnam vets—all these variants and more would present themselves in the neighborhood at any and all hours. At this unthinkably early hour, on this frigid morning in the middle of a bitter Chicago winter, our front door seemed to offer flimsy protection against whatever threat was on the other side.

Alarmed, I leapt out of bed, threw on some jeans, and yelled, "Who is it?" The voice came back, "CHICAGO POLICE! OPEN UP, OR I'M KICKING THE DOOR IN!"

The next few minutes or so are still a blur to me—but I am able to reconstruct most of the basic details.

DEA Special Agent John Zandy and an officer from the Chicago Police Department quickly stepped inside the opened door, announced that my roommate David and I were being arrested on the charge of "Sale of a Narcotic Substance," and ordered us both to present our hands forward to be handcuffed. 30 minutes later, we were being processed at the jail at 26th and California, and put into separate cells.

While in the back of the patrol car, I started piecing together how I had gotten into this mess.

★ ★ ★ ★

I first met my two apartment-mates, Peter and David, during our freshman year at University of Chicago. That first year at UC was something of a disappointment for me—and, I suspect, for my teachers. I had done very well on my entrance exams and, as a result, was placed into more advanced levels of the courses I most valued—namely, math and chemistry. After all, these were the courses that I had pictured as holding the key to my future. (Funny, right?)

The main reason I was so pleased with my performance on the tests was that I would now be able to swim with the big fish, instead of meandering about in the slower backwaters with the "deadwood." Yeah. Deadwood. You know—those poor souls who had to continually put their noses to the proverbial grindstone to get good grades. Unlike me, who had managed to sail through my high school courses without breaking a sweat.

However, I hadn't yet apprehended what would later seem so obvious—namely, that now that I was swimming with the big fish at UC, I would be expected to paddle hard to keep my head above water. To my great disappointment, the ability to even so much as break into a doggie paddle eluded me for my entire first year of school.

Of course, it wasn't like I was doing NOTHING that first year. I actually was quite busy with stuff that many college freshmen presumably do—things like making friends, reading a bunch of things that were not related to my actual courses, and "finding myself." The first pursuit mostly involved finding other musicians at school who were interested in the music I was interested in—that is, Chicago blues, as played in bars and clubs all over the South Side. By the second half of the year, I had acquired a fake ID through an older musician who had befriended me, which allowed me to get into the 43rd Street blues clubs, such as Pepper's and Theresa's, as well as places like the 1815 Club and Sylvio's on the West Side.

At that point, my search for musicians was no longer limited to school associations. Once that ID was in my wallet, these clubs were where I started spending as much time as I could.

Getting that fake ID was certainly my gateway to getting into—and soon afterwards, gigging in—Chicago's blues clubs. But the ease with which I was able to obtain the ID also exposed to me how things worked all over my hometown; whether on the street, in the courtrooms, or in the backrooms of power, everything could be had at a price, if you knew where to go and who to ask.

This generally cynical view of "the way things worked" was especially common in the Black community, which I was increasingly immersed in once I lived off-campus. One night, at a party during my second year at school, a hip-looking dude who I recognized from the music scene came up to me and said, "Hey, my man … I like the way you carry yourself." Once he had my attention, he said, "Lookie here. Do you know anyone who can hook me up?"

And, as a matter of fact, I did. My roommate David, an extremely bright and precocious fellow who had lived a somewhat sheltered life with his family in a wealthy Chicago suburb, had recently started dealing gingersnap-sized rounds of hashish, which he was getting direct from someone in Morocco. I gave the guy, who identified himself as Omar, our apartment's phone number and felt a glow of pleasure for having enhanced David's burgeoning customer base.

A few weeks later, the phone rang. An unfamiliar voice asked for David and, upon being informed that David wasn't home, said, "Hey, man, this is John. I'm a friend of Omar's, and he said David could hook us up for a party we're having tonight." I told him that David would be home later, but I wasn't sure when. John started to explain that the party just "wouldn't be the same" unless David could hook him up, and pressed me for specifics of when he could swing by. My protestations of inability to provide a time were met with more pleadings of "come on, dude … can't ya help a brother out?"

Finally, John said, "Hey, man … you know where he keeps his stash, right? Why don't you just hook us up yourself, from his stash, and we'll give you a little extra taste, on top of what we normally pay your buddy." Being fairly broke myself, and growing weary of resisting his pleas, I said, "Sure, come on over." A few minutes later, he did.

And that was the last I heard from or thought about John Zandy and his partner Omar until a few months later, when they knocked on our front door at 5:30AM on a frigid winter morning.

★ ★ ★ ★

The word among Sam Adam's colleagues was that he was one very odd duck—but an impressive lawyer.

The "odd duck" reputation stemmed from rumors that he lived in a predominantly black community on the South Side (and reportedly refused to reveal the location to anyone outside his family) despite the fact that his income certainly enabled him to live in a "nicer" neighborhood. For someone like me, that choice didn't appear "odd" at all. It was basically the same choice I myself had made—as had my parents during my childhood years.

The "impressive lawyer" part stemmed from his inclination to seek out cases pertaining to civil liberties and racial equity—often with the lofty intent of overturning oppressive laws and policies. Though it wasn't immediately clear how my legal predicament fit any of those descriptions, my dad was somehow able to arrange a meeting with Sam, in order to to discuss the charges against me, the penalties I might be facing, and whether he would be willing to take my case.

In most states, people arrested for a first offense of selling drugs like pot were typically allowed to plead guilty to a reduced charge of possession and given a light sentence. Perhaps even probation, without serving jail time. However, as Sam went on to explain, two factors made my own situation considerably more grave.

The first was the fact that under Illinois law, hashish, unlike pot, was considered to be a narcotic. And therefore, it was treated with the same legal severity as heroin, cocaine, and other "hard drugs."

The second was the fact that the political and racial climate in Chicago leading up to the 1968 Democratic Convention had just propelled a "law and order" candidate named Edward Hanrahan into office as Cook County States Attorney. Hanrahan will be remembered by most people for his role in the criminally one-sided police gun battle that killed Black Panther leaders Fred Hampton and Mark Clark in 1969, but his immediate effect on me personally was his campaign promise to eliminate all plea bargaining for drug offenders. If Hanrahan was to follow through on this campaign pledge—and refuse to bargain sale cases down to a guilty plea of possession—then I would be unable to avoid facing the charge of "sale of a narcotic substance." That charge carried a typical sentence of between two and ten years in Cook County Jail, without possibility of parole.

But … but … I WASN'T a drug dealer! My roommate DAVID was the drug dealer! I was just … well … helping out. Does that actually make me as guilty as the ACTUAL dealer?

Actually, as Sam explained—yes. It DOES.

But … but … I didn't WANT to make the sale! John Zandy PERSUADED me to make the sale that I didn't really want to do! Isn't that actually ENTRAPMENT?

Actually, as Sam further explained—no. It ISN'T.

The enormous consequences of my stupidity were hitting home very quickly, and very hard. As impressive a lawyer as Sam Adam apparently was, his calm, reasoned explanations of what I now was facing were simply too frightening to wrap my head around.

Like everyone, I had heard and read about what happens to people in inner-city jails—and as a physically small 19-year old white kid, I was frozen with terror. I had just returned from a trip to Mexico, and I immediately began speculating on where I could spend the rest of my life outside the US as a fugitive.

Sam certainly wasn't doing much to reassure my dad and me. But, were there really NO legal options? Wasn't there ANY way of fighting this?

Actually, Sam said, he DID have an idea. It was something he'd been thinking about for many years, in fact. It was something that he felt could—and SHOULD—be pushed through the judicial system. Something that he would be willing to sign on to, without asking any fee. But it represented a tremendous risk—a risk that would unfortunately be borne solely by me.

"You see," Sam began. "Illinois law presently allows a degree of latitude in sentencing for someone who pleads guilty to the sale of a narcotic. Typically, one to two years in jail, with possibility of parole even earlier than full term. However, if one pleads INNOCENT to the charge of sale—but is found GUILTY at trial—the law stipulates a mandatory ten-year sentence, without possibility of parole."

Warming to his point, Sam further explained, "This wide discrepancy in sentencing effectively forces many people, much like yourself, to plead guilty, even if they felt they had a case to make."

As Sam reached the crux of the argument that he had been turning over in his mind for several years, his voice rose in pitch and volume.

"And FORCING a defendant to plead guilty when they feel that they are INNOCENT," Sam thundered, "is exactly what the Fifth Amendment is designed to PROTECT against! I would LOVE to take a case based on that proposition all the way to the US Supreme Court. And, hopefully, we would succeed in getting this sentencing structure—this TRAVESTY of justice—CHANGED!"

For a moment, I was swept away by his fervor—and by the thought that my dad and I could partner with Sam to heroically effect change within a manifestly unjust system.

But ... what if we lose?

The look on Sam's face, and the weary shrug of his shoulders, was confirmation that my question was a rhetorical one. Sam Adam, my dad, and I all knew the answer already.

★ ★ ★ ★

The conventional wisdom for any criminal defense is to seek as many continuances as the court will allow—for a multitude of reasons.

For one, the more time that elapses after the date of commission of a crime, the more time a lawyer has to build a case that the client has taken steps to "turn their life around." (Shortly after agreeing to accept me as a client, Sam made it very clear to me that I would absolutely need to return to school, sever ties with my dealer friend David, cut my hair, and move out of the apartment where the sales had occurred.)

But in my particular case, the seeking of multiple continuances had another strategic function. As time went by, the hard-nosed "no plea bargains" promise that Hanrahan had ridden into office on would likely erode somewhat, and the DA's office might become a bit more flexible. Since I had basically choked at the idea of being the sacrificial guinea pig in Sam's grand scheme, an eventual plea bargain down to the charge of possession was really our best hope.

And sure enough, after several continuances were sought and granted, the possibility of a plea bargain with the DA's office was floated.

By now, almost a year and a half had gone by. I was back in school, ties with David had been severed, hair had been cut, and I was now living in a new apartment around the corner from my old one. Equally important, my case had gotten transferred to a Judge Kaufman—known to be a kindly man, and especially lenient to nice Jewish boys like myself. His lenience in my case took the form of allowing me to plead guilty to a charge of possession—still a felony by Illinois statute, but a damn sight better than what my prospects looked like 18 months earlier. My trial date was scheduled for the next month.

By the time of that final court date, Sam appeared fairly confident of what Judge Kaufman's decision would be. The "lengthy passage of time" between the original offense and the final trial—and Sam's apparently convincing argument for my "life turn-around"—were both mentioned in the judge's remarks, before he delivered his decision.

As my dad and I held our breaths, the verdict was read … three years probation, and no hard time.

★ ★ ★ ★

Truth be told, the imposition of three years of probation by the Cook County Department of Corrections was more than just a reprieve from the horrors of Cook County Jail. It actually proved to be a blessing in disguise, in its own right.

Over the years, I had employed various strategies for dodging the Vietnam War draft. The first was my 2S student deferment, which expired when I left school. Next was an attempt to reduce my weight to 113 and physically disqualify myself. And when that failed, I paid several visits to an anti-war shrink, resulting in a letter with a diagnosis of paranoid psychotic tendencies (which wound up scaring my dad, despite my warnings that the letter was merely a ruse). Eventually, it became clear that each strategy was only a temporary patch, and nothing more. My three-year probation sentence, however, proved to be the final fix.

The Cook County Correctional system's adamance in the face of pressure from the US Selective Service truly warmed the heart of this cowardly war objector. Their refusal to allow their charge to be removed from the probation program prevented me from being considered for military service until the draft was finally ended, two and a half years later.

Which just goes to prove the truth of that old adage from the '60s—"Every cloud of hashish smoke has a silver lining."

Magic Sam at the 1815 Club

Opening Up For Magic Sam

Have you ever been on the receiving end of an enthusiastic rave from someone who heard Springsteen and his band at the Stone Pony in Asbury Park, before they made it big? Or from someone who heard both Jimi Hendrix and Bob Dylan perform, before their first records dropped? (That would be me, actually, but each of those stories are covered elsewhere in this book).

Well, in that spirit, those of us lucky enough to hear Magic Sam at the Club Alex, the L&A Lounge, or other small clubs on West Madison Street knew we were hearing a guy who was primed to break nationally, and would bring real-deal, hard-edged Chicago blues to a larger, younger audience. After all—Sam had the voice, the looks, the stage presence, and a powerful "West-Side" guitar style that couldn't remain Chicago's best-kept secret forever.

Sadly, Sam died in December, 1969 of a heart attack at age 32, as he was literally on the brink of stardom. Ten years later, the mantle was passed to another "brown-eyed handsome man," with all the same things going for him that Sam had. That young man's name was Robert Cray—a guy who deserves everything he's achieved in the decades since. But if Sam hadn't passed in '69, I'm confident that we'd all be talking about Magic Sam in the same way we talk about Robert Cray.

One day around 1968, I got a call from Sam, who said he needed a rhythm guitar player for a gig at a spot on 63rd Street on the South Side, around 10 blocks from my house. Was I available? Hell, yeah, I was available!

However, I couldn't help but wonder, "Why does Sam need a rhythm guitar player?." If there EVER was a guy who could generate enough self-sufficient, guitar-

driven "oomph" on his own, it was Sam Maghett. And although he occasionally recorded with a rhythm guitarist, I had never seen him use one live. But I certainly wasn't going to say "no" to the gig.

I showed up at the gig early, loaded in my stuff, and, shortly thereafter, other guys from the band started drifting in. But no Sam.

So, where on the stage should I set up? Eventually, I chose a logical-looking spot, off to the side, leaving the center stage for the main attraction. But still no Sam.

Hmmm.

Shortly before showtime, the room had almost entirely filled with people, all eagerly awaiting the MAN. And at that point, Sam came in through a side door with his guitar and amp, made his way through the crowd to the stage, and greeted everyone in the band. I was the last one he said hello to.

Leaving Theresa's

Sam turned to me and said, "Are you ready to go?" I indicated I was—tuned and ready. Then Sam said, "Good. So, start off with a couple of tunes, get the place warmed up, and then bring me up."

That's when it hit me.

Sam didn't need a rhythm guitar player. What he had here was a better-than-average-paying gig. So what he wanted was to sit back and let the band start the show before the headliner gets announced and brought to the stage with a bunch of fanfare—a showbiz formula that I had seen countless times in clubs. Of course! Why didn't I see this coming?

The only problem was that I had never really prepared a bunch of tunes to sing on my own, which I would now pull out of a hat on the spur of this exact moment. Nor had I really premeditated the kind of signals and body English necessary to lead the band through my "tune arrangements." And I CERTAINLY hadn't prepared myself to be the self-assured, charismatic MC that Sam obviously hoped he'd hired.

So what did I do? Honestly, I don't remember.

But I suspect I played a couple of Freddie King tunes, a jazz-inflected instrumental or two, and presumably managed to pull off an announcement of the man everyone had come to see—the sensation-maker—the record-breaker—the sensational West Side Soul man, MAGIC SAM!

I'm glad iPhones weren't around back then. I'm sure I'd CRINGE to see what sort of announcement I'd made, in return for the money Sam paid me.

Sam Maghett was born in 1932 and died in 1969. Had he lived, he would be 87 years old today. I can't help but think of how much poorer the music world is for his leaving us so prematurely. Sam, I hope you've got that rhythm guitar player/MC you so richly deserve, in that glorious blues band you're fronting up yonder!

Howlin' Wolf

"The London Howlin' Wolf Sessions," and Sausage-Making

Fifty-four years ago, a bunch of popular young British blues musicians gathered at Olympic Studios in London in order to record with an icon of Chicago Blues, Howlin' Wolf. 15 months later, the tracks they recorded were released on Chess Records as *The London Howlin' Wolf Sessions*. A lot of things occurred in that 15-month period, which I'll shed a bit of light on, for those interested in such things—including the backstory behind one particular tune, "I Ain't Superstitious."

Full disclosure. For anyone who likes sausage—but doesn't want to know how it's actually made—you might want to stop reading now!

In 1967 or so, I started playing in a blues/R&B band started by harp player and vocalist Jeff Carp. It was a large band of all top-notch players, including a three to four horn section. (Several of the players have continued on to respectable pro career, in genres ranging from R&B to Jazz to Classical—in settings ranging from NYC studios and major jazz festivals to the Juilliard String Quartet.)

In addition to that band, Jeff and I stayed tight for a number of years, playing and touring with

The Jeff Carp Band

bands led by Earl Hooker and Sam Lay, and doing a bunch of recording sessions together with artists like John Lee Hooker, Earl Hooker, Lightnin' Hopkins, etc. Jeff's original band caught the eye of producer and blues documentarian Norman Dayron, who recorded us at Chess Studios in hopes of following in Blood, Sweat & Tears' wake and arranging a record contract for the band. More (MUCH more!) about Norman can be found in the story entitled "Killin' The Blues… The Most Bizarre Recording Session in History."

It was during that same period of time that Norman persuaded Marshall Chess to make a record pairing high-profile white blues players like Paul Butterfield and Mike Bloomfield with their musical father, Muddy Waters, in order to create a larger market for Mud. Projects of that nature often turn out poorly—but the project that emerged, *Fathers and Sons*, was a terrific record, and was well-received by fans of the fathers AND sons alike. A lot of the success of the project was due to choosing the perfect lineup of musicians, including Muddy's longtime pianist Otis Spann, bassist Duck Dunn, and drummer Sam Lay. Since Jeff and I were already working regularly in Sam's band, we were considered good fits to round out the lineup.

Upon the success of *Fathers and Sons*, Norman and Marshall Chess hatched an idea for a followup—this time with Howlin' Wolf as featured "father," and British icons like Eric Clapton and Steve Winwood as "sons." For logistical reasons, London was decided as the location, and Jeff was tapped to play harp on the project, since Wolf was then in poor health.

London Howlin' Wolf Session

However, unlike the *Fathers and Sons* project, the *London Howlin' Wolf Sessions* was something of a clusterfuck—and when the tracks were brought back to Chicago, many of them sounded pretty disappointing. Clapton and Winwood did fine work, as one would expect. But much of the rhythm section playing was inept and lacked the groove and feel of the Chicago players, such as Sam Lay, Jerome Arnold, S.P. Leary, and Andrew McMahon, who played regularly in Wolf's band. And when measured by the standard of the original recordings produced at Chess—well, let's just say it made for an unflattering comparison.

By this time, Norman felt that Jeff and I had chalked up a respectable track record of studio accomplishments, and he had grown to trust and value our experience and opinions regarding the music. Consequently, he allowed us to make a number of decisions regarding the album's arrangements—some of them relatively minor, but some of them more radical. Here's an example of the latter.

In order to help perform a groove transfusion on some of the tracks, we overdubbed veteran bassist (as well as terrific guitarist) Phil Upchurch on several tunes. This is a relatively commonplace occurrence in this day and age of Pro Tools, virtual instruments, click tracks, and trans-Atlantic pop collaborations. But in the '60s, at Chess Studios, this was a pretty daring leap.

Nevertheless, the leap paid off. 'Church had always been a total pro, and a couple of hours later, the tracks were rescued. Mission accomplished. On to the next tasks.

One track in particular required no such repair, but it was considered less exciting than it could be. "I Ain't Superstitious" had an unobjectionable groove, with Clapton playing the repetitive figure with great Strat tone and feel. But the tune seemed to suggest so much more excitement than was actually achieved in the track. Plus, it had an inexplicably long rideout that never really built steam.

Two options presented themselves. Either chop off most of the rideout by fading the track out early—which seemed a waste, and would create an unsatisfyingly short tune as a result—or beef up the track with additional percussion, and overdub a horn section that would build incrementally over the course of the last several minutes. Since our band had a kick-ass horn section that specialized in exactly that approach, we chose the latter option and concocted an arrangement to gradually kick up the track with each chorus.

Once done, however, we realized a problem. Clapton's guitar part, though played really nicely, now appeared underwhelming in contrast to the dynamic horn section. Had the horns been there on the original session, he clearly would have been answering the horn figures with searing lead licks. But since they WEREN'T there, those spaces now sounded empty.

The Jeff Carp Band

So I was tapped to be Clapton, and fill them. I borrowed my friend's Strat and had fun riffing away, starting at 2:40. After a few passes, we got what was needed.

In the essay "Puppet Shows, and The Producer," I ruminate a bit on the role production plays in the magic of musical recording. With that thought in mind—was the Howlin' Wolf track "overproduced" as a result of our efforts?

I'll leave that up to others to decide.

When all the work on the album was done, Norman reminded me of an agreement we had made before embarking on the project. He didn't want too many musicians' names in the credits out of concern that it would overshadow the "headliners." So, my name wound up in the "Special Thanks To" section, along with Mick Jagger, Ahmet Ertegun, Ian Stewart, and others.

And THAT'S how sausage is made!

Engineer: Glyn Johns
Recorded: Olympic Sound Studios, London, England
Re-mixed: RCA Studios, Chicago, Illinois
Mastered: Sterling Sound, New York, New York
Album Design: The Daily Planet
Illustration: Don Wilson
Session Photos: Jo McDermand
Inside Cover Photo: Peter Amft

Special Thanks to:
  Mick Jagger, Ian Stewart, Marshall Chess,
  Ahmet Ertegun, Robert Stigwood,
  Chris Blackwell, John Eastman, Bob Ludwig,
  Erwin Helfer, Peter J. Welding, Paul Asbell,
  Joel Smirnoff, and Be-Bop Sam

Eric Clapton appears courtesy of Robert Stigwood Organization, Ltd.
Steve Winwood appears courtesy of Island Records, Ltd.
Bill Wyman and Charlie Watts appear courtesy of Rolling Stones Records, Ltd.

PRODUCED BY NORMAN DAYRON
A Holy Smoke Production

A Song For Sam Cooke

In 1961, I was living a musical double-life. A few years earlier, I had discovered some of the 78s and LPs in my dad's record collection—Woody Guthrie, Blind Willie Johnson, John Lee Hooker, the Staples Singers, Flatt & Scruggs, etc.—and had been trying to figure out why I was drawn to THESE records instead of the Top 40 music that most of my friends listened to on the radio.

Sure, there were obvious differences in their musical style. Differences that I intuitively recognized but didn't quite have the vocabulary to describe. But these records of my dad's also seemed to contain more emotional "meat" to them—more grit and less artifice, more passion and less silliness—than what I heard on the radio. Somehow, the songs on these records just seemed more "genuine."

Unlike the music my friends were listening to, it seemed like the songs on these records of my dad's were making statements. Statements that, for some reason, really spoke to me.

But as much as I didn't want to admit it at the time, there WERE some songs that caught my ear, and caused little bursts of excitement and involuntary bodily twitches, whenever the first notes came over the loudspeaker of my little homemade radio. One of them was a tune called "Mother In Law" by a guy whose name I learned later was Ernie K-Doe. Another was "A Quarter to Three" by Gary US Bonds. Others included "Shop Around" by the Miracles, "Raindrops" by Dee Clark, "I Like it Like That" by Chris Kenner, "Hit The Road, Jack" by Ray Charles, "Mama Said" by the Shirelles, "Stand By Me" by Ben E. King, and a couple of songs—"The Wanderer" and "Runaround Sue"—by a guy who apparently had just one name. Dion.

Though I clearly enjoyed the feeling whenever these songs came on the radio, my mind knew better—and placed them squarely into the category of frivolous "kid stuff." Which, as I write this now, strikes me as pretty funny. After all, I was only twelve—which probably explains why I never spent a lot of mental energy reflecting on the common denominator those songs possessed that caused those little bursts of excitement and those twitches.

All I knew was that there was SOMETHING very different about those songs than, say, "Does Your Chewing Gum Lose Its Flavor On the Bedpost Overnight?" or "Where the Boys Are"—songs that surfed the very same airwaves and flew into my radio at the very same spot on my AM radio dial.

It was many, many years before I figured out what it was about the singers, the rhythm tracks, and the overall grooves that defined them and caught my ear. But at that time, I was like certain sanctimoniously conservative pundits are on the radio today, I guess.

Evidently, I didn't HEAR color.

Yeah, Paul—but what about Dion? His real name was Dion DiMucci, and he was (and still is) WHITE. Why did HE fit into that "involuntary twitches" category?

Well, like I said—I was twelve at the time, and had no idea then about the apparently racial metrics underlying my double life and my emotional reactions to the music. All I knew was that, despite the inherently shallow lyrics of the songs coming out of my radio speaker, this music had something that I really liked.

Several years later, of course, this Dion guy came out with a song called "Abraham, Martin, and John." By then, I was FULLY aware of the racial dynamics of both the world I lived in and the music I was instinctively drawn towards. So I was now completely aware of the statement Dion was making by releasing that song.

In May 2020, while COVID locked down much of our nation and paralyzed the entire music business, Dion went into a recording studio and recorded "Song For Sam Cooke (Here In America)." The YouTube video of it is quite interesting because it starts out with an off-the-cuff verbal introduction—just like a live performer might do on stage—and then a somewhat shaky false start of the song, followed by a quick clearing of his throat, as if the emotion of the tune's message temporarily got the better of him. But then, the band

kicks in behind him, and he delivers the song with all cylinders firing. The video subtly turns from color to black and white as he sings the song's first line, "We traveled this land back in 1962," while similarly subtle but effective "Ooh-Ahh"s (provided by Paul Simon) make explicit the connection to Sam's ground-breaking protest song "Chain Gang." The lyrics evoke a time when Dion and Sam toured the South, playing shows and dodging the

Dion DiMucci

ubiquitous, overt racism that was everywhere around them. And, in the process, Dion pays homage to the friendship he and Sam enjoyed together, through it all.

As I listened, I reflected on my own musical "double life" back in 1962. Back then, I was trying to reconcile my admiration for music that "felt genuine" with my attraction to music that simply "felt good." With this song for Sam Cooke, however, Dion managed to squarely hit both targets.

His vocal delivery here is utterly natural, yet contains just the right touch of soulful grit, without any of the artifice common to white singers trying to "sing Black." Through his unforced singing, the song's message is firmly driven home—the double life our nation was ALSO living during those early years of the civil rights struggle, while "Does Your Chewing Gum Lose Its Flavor On the Bedpost Overnight?" and "Where the Boys Are" were playing on America's AM radios.

Dion's apparently not done making statements. Despite the brief false start at the beginning of this recording, Dion, like Bob Dylan, shows that he knows his song well before he starts singing. Respect, my man!

Puppet Shows, and The Producer

In 2016, George Martin, "the fifth Beatle"—and arguably the most famous record producer who ever lived—passed away at the age of 90.

But, before telling you about George, and about what record producers do, allow me to tell you a little story about myself.

★ ★ ★ ★

At age seven, my parents noticed that I was acquiring a lot of bruises that never seemed to heal properly. True, kids do a lot of things that cause bruises. But this was different—a fact that was eventually borne out by medical tests. And, so began a long six months of painful procedures, extended stays at Michael Reese hospital, and, ultimately, an operation to remove my spleen.

One day, while recuperating in the hospital, my dad came to visit and took me to a puppet show that was taking place several floors below. I sat in the front row with the other kids, with my dad sitting awkwardly next to me, obviously restless at having to sit patiently through the show. A few minutes into the show, my dad got up and walked over to the side of the room. A minute later, he returned to his seat and whispered in my ear, "Paul—do you want to go over to the side of the stage, and see how the puppets work?" I must have looked at him quizzically, because he began to explain that there were people behind the tiny stage making the puppets work with their hands, and that you could actually SEE them from the corner of the room that he had just come from.

I remember being torn, because I really wanted to be sitting there with my dad—who never visited the hospital as much as I wished he did. So I certainly didn't want to discourage him from visiting again by appearing ungrateful for the time he spent with me.

But I also really didn't want to go the side of the room with him and watch how the guys were operating the puppets. I mean—how could you enjoy watching the puppet show, after you saw the artifice of how the show actually worked?

So, I stayed in my seat and watched the puppets, transported by the magic of the story.

★ ★ ★ ★

At age 18, I started playing in clubs in my South Side Chicago neighborhood, alongside older men who had previously been childhood heroes. There were many exhilarating moments on stage with these iconic figures, who I once only knew from the covers of record albums.

However, along with the exhilaration came uncomfortable realizations. Men who had recorded some of the most powerful, riveting music I had ever heard were now here, next to me, sandwiching vapid jukebox hits between their powerful blues numbers. I couldn't understand why they felt the need to "play to the people"—and after my naive, adolescent eyes were opened to the simple fact that these men were just trying to make a living, I struggled with how to view my former heroes in the same idealized light that I had two years earlier.

The answer I gradually came to was this. I couldn't. The music I so dearly loved seemed to take on new and different meanings now that I was seeing it from the vantage point of the guy on stage. I felt that very soon, I would have to make a decision. I could hold onto my fantasy of what I imagined the blues to be—which meant I'd have to stop playing with all my heroes—or I could choose to look at the music world I was gradually moving into with eyes wide open.

Which one's it gonna be, Paul … the fantasy, or the reality? You can't have both. But this time around, I chose differently than I did when I was seven.

For better or worse, I chose the reality of being a professional musician. And gradually, I began to realize that the magic in the music didn't disappear—even when viewed from behind the scenes, where one sees all the angles of how the show actually works.

★ ★ ★ ★

Around this time, I began getting calls to play studio sessions. Many of them were at the iconic Chess Studios, the hallowed ground where Muddy Waters, Howlin' Wolf, Otis Rush, and Buddy Guy recorded. By then, I was fairly aware of the fact that the music world, as viewed from backstage, was not quite as glamorous as the view from the front row seats made it appear. So, I was not especially surprised that the studios' appearance was quite mundane.

What DID surprise me, however, was how the sessions were conducted in these mundane rooms. I imagined magic moments of lightning captured in a bottle. But instead, the process seemed more like making a movie—short bursts of actual band music-making, interspersed with longer periods of technical adjustments, and arguments over arrangements—all accompanied by disheartening displays of every frailty and failing of which the human ego is capable.

Was this how my favorite Chess blues recordings were made? It certainly wasn't what I had imagined, listening to them as a young teen, five years earlier. But the more I watched and participated in these sessions during the late '60s, the more I began to suspect the answer was "yes."

Clearly, some sort of magic must be taking place on a regular basis, in order to bring forth from these haphazard recording sessions an exciting, tight-sounding, cohesive record. And by having the opportunity to watch men like Willie Dixon, Gene Barge, and Charles Stepney at work, I began to realize what that "magic" was.

It was called "production."

George Martin with The Beatles

★ ★ ★ ★

Which brings us back to record producer George Martin.

As he was for practically every recording artist in the world, George was a hero to me and my bandmates in the Unknown Blues Band. The string arrangements, the classical music flourishes, the remarkable juxtapositions of those sophisticated elements with the edgy rock and avant-garde sensibilities of the tracks they embellished—these details were all immediately apparent to me and my musician friends, made all the more impressive by the fact that they were so unremarked on by the general public.

Upon hearing of his death, I immediately thought of the time in the mid-'80s when we were asked to play at the wedding of George's son, Greg. The opportunity to meet the man who had taken the Beatles' lightning in a bottle—and alchemically combined them with his own very different skills to craft all those iconic recordings—was exhilarating.

But … what was he actually like? Would the man who produced the Beatles, Elton John, Pete Townsend, and Dire Straits want to take time from his own son's wedding to hang out with a bunch of less-than-household-name musicians? And what if he turned out to be a self-absorbed jerk?

Well, he wasn't. In fact, he was a wonderful cat, who clearly enjoyed talking endless peer-to-peer shop with musicians who he obviously had never heard of.

Yes, of course, there were a few Beatles stories that cropped up in the conversation. Being someone like George Martin means you can never not be "that guy."

But what I most remember is his delight in talking about his work with *The Goon Show*, a BBC comedy show that featured Peter Sellers and Dudley Moore, and was considered to be the forerunner to Monty Python. To hear his delight in telling those *Goon Show* stories, you'd think that it was the highlight of his entire career.

Who knows … maybe it was?

A truly lovely man. Rave on, George Martin, wherever you are.

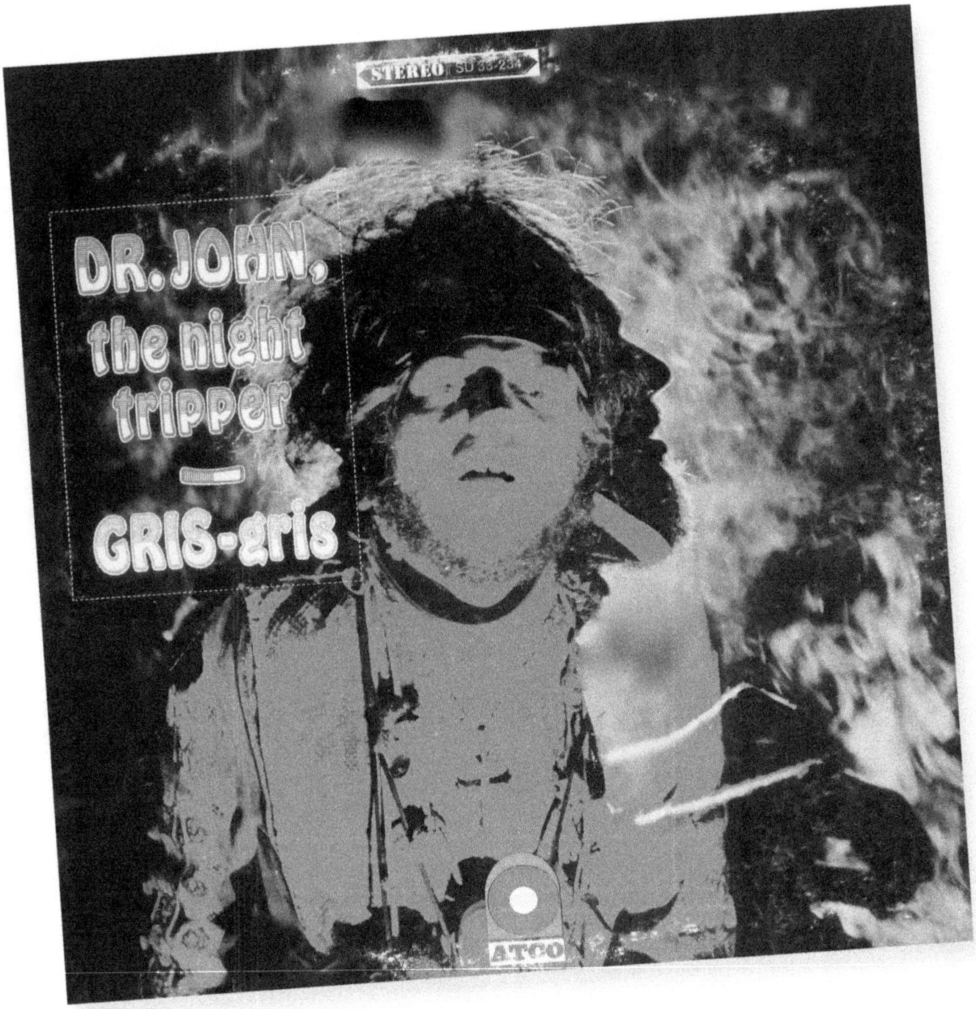
STEREO SD 33-234
DR. JOHN,
the night
tripper
GRIS-gris
ATCO

The Trickonology
Master Hisself

I remember browsing the bins of a record store (remember THOSE?) one day in 1968, and seeing an odd-looking cover by an artist called "Dr. John, the Night Tripper." Since I was pretty deeply into Chicago-style blues and R&B at the time—and the cover photo seemed to suggest more of a psychedelic soundscape than funky music—I chuckled and kept flipping through.

Months later, I heard "Walk On Gilded Splinters" at a friend's house and realized there was more to this act than a weird getup, pot smoke and mirrors. The atmospherics that New Orleans-turned-LA producer Harold Battiste draped around the band's hypnotic grooves got deeply under my skin, and alerted me to the fact that soul-affecting music could come in many more forms than a field holler, a gospel shout, or a blues shuffle.

Around that time, I began hearing that the character at the center of this Voodoo-drenched theatrical presentation was also a New Orleans expatriate—a guitarist-turned-pianist named Mac Rebennack.

Much later, I heard from fellow musicians that Mac was NOT the original guy who was tapped for the "Dr. John" role in this theatrical enterprise. The original man for whom the character was tailored was R&B singer and keyboardist Ronnie Barron—but as is often the case in the musical world, "health issues" at the last minute prevented Barron from participating, and Mac reluctantly agreed to fill in as understudy for the role.

And that's how session musician and studio producer Mac Rebennack came to be known to the world at large as Dr. John.

It wasn't until I heard the album *Gumbo* in 1972 that I fully appreciated the piano skills that the man possessed, those which undergirded his live performances. Mac's piano skills were a crucial ingredient in his composition "Such A Night," which was released in 1973. That song was solidified as a signature for Mac after its inclusion in the music documentary *The Last Waltz*, and he subsequently performed the tune until the end of his career.

Like virtually all artistic phenomena, Mac's style began as an extension of the musical world he grew up in—in his case, New Orleans R&B. His piano skills were a direct extension of a style pioneered by his NOLA homie Roy Byrd—a man eventually known to the larger world as Professor Longhair. Once I realized how deep into the musical earth of New Orleans his roots actually descended, I became a wholehearted Mac Rebennack fan, and remain one to this day.

I worked up an arrangement of Mac's tune "Such A Night" for my *Steel String Americana* CD, which I recorded in 2002. The challenge of making Mac's piano tour-de-force come alive on guitar was a great one for me, and singing on top of it took a while to comfortably dial in. I'm glad I did, though, as it's become an audience favorite and the lead-off tune for many of my shows.

Mac was born in 1940 and passed on in 2019. He left the world a fantastic legacy of New Orleans funk, second-line chants, and the original tunes he brewed up out of those savory ingredients. And, of course, a uniquely personal spoken-word art form he called "trickonology," which he employed to generate a library of hysterically memorable quotes on music, culture, his hometown, and life in general.

He now resides in heaven at the right hand of the father, next to the drummer's hi-hat. Hope they're makin' the Red Beans the way you like 'em up there, Mac!

"I'll Just Sit Here and Do What I Do"

In 1969, the man who I described in my earlier story "Guitar Heroes"—legendary Chicago blues guitarist Earl Hooker— asked me and my partner-in-crime, harmonica ace Jeff Carp, if we wanted to do a California tour with him.

At the time, Jeff and I were working in Sam Lay's band—so we anticipated that saying "yes" to Earl's offer would displease Sam, and have unpredictable repercussions. On the other hand, Earl lived near us on the South Side, and worked at South Side clubs like Pepper's Lounge regularly—whereas Sam lived on the West Side, and exhibited a mysterious antipathy to booking gigs at Pepper's and other South Side clubs. After a few late evenings spent pondering the question, Jeff and I decided to accept Earl's offer, and began to get excited about the California adventure.

The plan was to set out for the West Coast in Earl's converted Cadillac hearse, which he used for all his road trips. The hearse had enough room for the guitars, amps, a set of drums, and the band itself—Earl, pianist John "Big Moose" Walker, bassist Geno Skaggs, drummer Roosevelt Shaw, vocalist Andrew "Little BB" Odom, Jeff, and me. Tight quarters for seven guys to travel over 2000 miles in … but on the other hand, we'd certainly get to know one another better by the time we got to the coast.

Four days before we were set to leave, however, Earl called to report a snag. Apparently, he had parked his hearse the night before in an alley around 3300 W. Flournoy on the West Side, and when he went out the next morning, he found the hearse had burnt up, and was now nothing but a smoking pile of rubble.

Upon hearing the address Earl had parked at, Jeff and I looked at one another and began to giggle like little kids. What we knew, but Earl apparently didn't, was that 3300

W. Flournoy was the block that Sam lived on. A remarkable coincidence, indeed ... but one which we were certainly not about to point out to Earl. But what would now happen with the plans for a tour?

Well, Earl managed to find another converted Cadillac hearse. (How many of these things WERE there? And how did Earl find another one so quickly? So many questions never asked and, as a result, never answered.) But within two days, the plans for the tour were back in full effect, and two days after that, we set off for California.

After a long, wild trip traversing the continent, we made it to the West Coast, played a number of dates in San Francisco and the Bay Area, and then headed south to Los Angeles. There, we played several relatively high-profile clubs, included one on Sunset Strip where a new up-and-coming rock group calling themselves "The Doors" had just played.

While in LA, Earl was approached by ABC-Bluesway to do a couple of recordings. The first one we recorded, "Don't Have To Worry," was discussed in the earlier piece.

But the second one was even more tantalizing to me because it represented an opportunity to work with a man whose records I used to fall asleep listening to as a young teen—Earl's cousin, John Lee Hooker. That record, named for a story-song John Lee conjured up about him and his cousin Earl in a fanciful "43rd Street-meets-High-Noon" setting, came out a few months later as *If You Miss Him, I Got Him.*

As was typical of blues recording sessions back in that day, that second session went fairly quickly, and we managed to get five tunes down on tape, each of which fulfilled the producer's hopes for a musical "hangout session" of the two cousins. At that point, we all took a break before putting the last four tunes in the can, and meandered downstairs to a record shop at street level, directly below the upstairs studio.

Although we had already played several hours of music together, this was the first opportunity for some of us to relax and get to know John Lee "off-camera." Unsurprisingly, the man was as relaxed, down-to-earth, and real "off-set" as he was while the tape was rolling.

Once in the shop, we all made a beeline to the blues section and started pawing through the record bins (an admittedly vintage reference to a bygone era, during which people read essays like this by the light of whale-oil lamps.) The store was unusually well-stocked, allowing us to check out the new releases of fellow artists, older legends, and newer faces on the scene.

While casually looking over our shoulders at the record covers, John Lee started reminiscing in a quiet voice about the artists he knew and had worked with over the decades. In the midst of a story about a younger artist he had recently worked with, John Lee looked up at the wall, on which hung a poster of Muddy Waters wearing a toga outfit—a marketing scheme cooked up by a then-young Marshall Chess to promote the new LP *Electric Mud* to the rock world.

John Lee looked at the picture, chuckled, and said under his breath to no one in particular, "Look what they got Mud doin' now."

Muddy Waters

No outrage, no resentment or jealousy—just a bit of worldly-wise amusement at the marketing world's never-ending quest for novelty. And for a brief moment, the 19-year-old that I was got a brief glimpse of what a lifelong career in music looked like, through the eyes of one of my all-time musical heroes.

John Lee Hooker

Many years later, a friend and I were chatting about the experience that afternoon. After reflecting on the story, and my impressions of John Lee's Zen-like perspective on the "fame game," my buddy said wistfully, "I hope he had a good life."

Which got me thinking about that hope, and the larger questions raised. Questions which I've increasingly come to turn over in my mind through the act of writing.

An obvious disclaimer. There's no way that someone like me could truly know the answer to my friend's comment. But here's my guess.

I suspect he DID have a pretty good life—especially compared to many of his peers.

I don't think his expectations of life involved plans for world domination, marketing schemes to turn the world onto his music, sweating where his records charted, worrying about the next tour, or the ups and downs of his career arc. I think his life was kinda like his entire musical presentation format … "I'll just sit here and do what I do, and I'll be doing that whether you're behind me or not."

And for what—over five decades?—it pretty much worked for him. After all, John Lee Hooker was quite the hitmaker, and a star in the Black community going back to the late '40s—decades before a new generation of white listeners discovered and enthusiastically embraced his music in the '60s.

So, yeah. All things considered—and at the risk of sounding insensitive and clueless—I believe he DID have a pretty good life.

John Lee was born in 1920 (though it's often speculated that the actual year was 1912, or 1915, or 1917, or 1923). But whatever year he was born, once the man started recording his music, he left an indelible mark on American popular culture that continues to this day, and will undoubtedly last for a long time to come.

Here's my shoutout to a transcendent Mississippi-born bluesman—a man who started out rocking small clubs on Hasting Street in Detroit, Michigan and eventually built a legendary international career that he rode into his 80s—the one and only John Lee Hooker.

Counterweight

The neighborhood I grew up in, the values of my parents, the sounds in the air I instinctively gravitated towards—all these influences left a profound stamp on who I am. I've tried to examine some of these influences in the essays found in this book—"A Benefit Concert, On a School Night," "A Song For Sam Cooke," and "Cardboard Boxes, and Origin Stories" come immediately to mind.

In my late teens, I made the "decision" to forge a career in music. But it would be just as accurate to say the decision made me. 56 years later, I can reflect on how much I'm indebted to those music influences—for the opportunity I've had to occasionally stand on the shoulders of giants, and to learn the skills necessary to play my own music in their footsteps.

The music I chose (or, perhaps, the music that chose ME) is Black American Music. Blues, Jazz, R&B, Soul music—many flavors, but they're all rooted in the Black American experience and were a folk music for black people, well before white people like myself found their way into the mix. As I see it, being allowed into that mix is an honor and an implied debt that I'll be paying for the rest of my life.

I have many, many friends who have felt the same tug of gravity, and have forged careers around playing this music. All of us who have done so also know our society's shameful social and economic exploitation of the architects and icons of it. With that in mind, I'd like to make a personal exhortation to all of you.

In November 2016, 26 percent of our nation's citizens voted to usher in a political climate of rejection of the interests of Black people and Black culture, unlike any time since the 1950s. This rejection was repeated in November 2024. I feel strongly that those of us whose lives have been enriched by Black culture have a moral obligation to

Frederick Douglass

forcefully and consistently speak and act as counterweights to this exploitation. To do anything less than that is to implicitly reap the benefits of all the exploitation that has gone on before.

Each of us can find our way to do this, and we certainly won't speak with one ideological voice when we do. But to remain silent, in order to avoid alienating potential fans, venues, or employment institutions, is NOT an option, in my opinion.

As the great Frederick Douglass posted recently on Facebook, "You either have to be part of the solution, or you're going to be part of the problem."

That, of course, was a joke. But the moral imperative to be a counterweight ISN'T.

Jimmy Driftwood

Arkansas Travelers

When I was aged 11 (though the exact date is in question, depending on which version of family lore one subscribes to) my parents, brothers, and I piled into our green Studebaker and drove south from our home in Chicago to rural Arkansas. Our destination was the home of a schoolteacher named James Morris, who wrote songs under the *nom de plume* Jimmy Driftwood.

Mr. Morris (as I presume his students called him) took both his educational mission and the folklore of his region equally to heart. So, when called upon to teach his students about a then-125-year-old topic like the War of 1812, he did what any songwriter would be expected to do—he wrote songs about it.

One song in particular concerned a battle that occurred weeks after a peace treaty had already been signed by British and American negotiators in Europe. However, since news of the signing hadn't reached the US—and the US Congress hadn't yet ratified the treaty—the battle was fought, leading to a rousing victory for the ragtag US army of Appalachian settlers, Acadian refugees living in the swamps of central Louisiana, free men of color, Choctaw Indians, pirates under the command of Jean Lafitte, and various uniformed US troops—all assembled under the command of General Andrew Jackson.

The lyrics Mr. Morris came up with for his history lesson contained exactly the sort of humor and bravado that 10-year-old school kids could be expected to fall in love with, and sing lustily at recess, on Boy Scout hikes, or around campfires late in the evening. He chose an old fiddle tune known as "The 8th of January" to drape his new lyrics over, based on the fact that the battle itself had been fought on that exact date in 1815.

The song he came up with remained a strictly local favorite for 20 years until the opportunity presented itself to record it in Nashville in 1957. That session in turn led to a recording contract for Jimmy. However, due to the inclusion of colorful language like "hell" and "damn," Jimmy's recorded version couldn't be played on the radio.

Jimmy was later fond of joking that those very words could be regularly shouted from the pulpit, but couldn't be broadcast over the radio airwaves.

A year later, Nashville producer and master guitarist Chet Atkins brought the song to the attention of a pop singer named Johnny Horton. Horton, with the assistance and expertise of veteran producer Don Law (the very same guy who had recorded Mississippi bluesman Robert Johnson in a hotel room in San Antonio in 1936, creating a series of recordings that inspired British blues-rock icons Eric Clapton and Keith Richards 30 years later) made a #1 Top 40 hit out of it.

And that, my friends, is how everyone's childhood sing-a-long favorite, "The Battle of New Orleans," became Billboard's longest-charting national airplay song for the year 1959. (Hint, for those who think they don't remember it. It begins with the line "In 1814 we took a little trip...")

Later in that same year of '59, my dad was hired to a write a magazine article about this curious example of authentic grassroots Americana getting recycled into the Top 40 mainstream of American pop culture—a foreshadowing of the *O, Brother, Where Art Thou* sensation 40 years later. And that's why my parents, my two brothers and I piled into our green Studebaker and drove the 580 miles of red-clay roads to the tiny town of Timbo, Arkansas to meet Jimmy Driftwood and his wife Cleda.

However, we didn't all actually STAY with Jimmy and Cleda.

You see, while my dad and mom stayed at the Driftwood's small cabin in Timbo for a week or so, my brothers and I were placed in a horse camp in the nearby town of Mountain View. There, I was expected to learn to groom and take care of an animal weighing 20 times my own weight, which was fairly intimidating for a kid who up to that point had experienced very little of the earthy realities of country living. But even more intimidating was the prospect of having to use the smelly, communal outhouse for ten days, which was the only form of waste management available on the ranch.

Looking back on my visceral response to that outhouse, I can see now that what I did was a foreshadowing of a lifelong approach to unthinkable, insurmountable challenges. I simply refused to go into the damn thing, let alone USE it. Any intuitive understanding I might have had about the function of poops in the grand biological design was handily overcome by my stubborn determination to ignore the challenge altogether.

Several weeks later, on the ride home, I started complaining of feeling light-headed. By the time we got home to Chicago, it was clear to my mother that I really WAS sick. I was running a fever, and the lightheadedness had progressed into full-blown delirium.

My immediate concern upon getting home, however, was not my delirium, but rather an urgent desire to run upstairs and make sure that my two white mice pets were OK. To my shock and horror, they were NOT OK. Lying there on the wood shavings at the bottom of their little cage lay one of the mice, which appeared to be dead. And the other one was nowhere to be found.

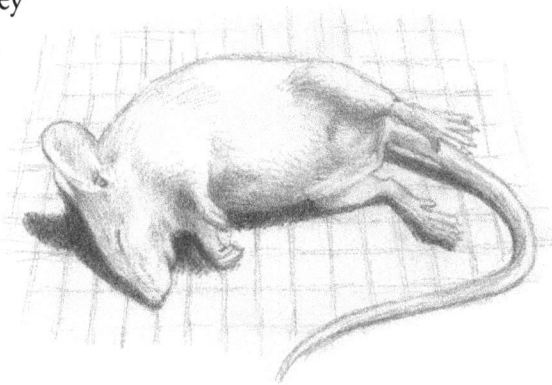

I couldn't understand how ALL of the food I had generously provided for the two weeks we planned to be gone had disappeared. How had they managed to eat that much, in such a short time? And how could the OTHER mouse have possibly managed to escape the cage where they both had lived for months? There certainly didn't appear to be any way that a mouse could possibly have wiggled through the bars.

And then, it hit me. It hit me with such insurmountable force that I was utterly unable to ignore the explanation for what clearly had happened.

A hero from somewhat later in my childhood, Sherlock Holmes, was fond of schooling his dutiful chronicler Watson that "when you have eliminated the impossible, whatever remains, however improbable, must be the truth." And so it is with caged white mice. The improbable—nay, the unthinkable, the MONSTROUS, insurmountable conclusion—must be the truth. The irrefutable, unignorable truth.

And with that monstrous image of my dead mice flashing like a horrible skull-and-crossbones neon sign in front of my eyes, I suddenly lurched down the hall to the bathroom, my mother close behind me, and vomited whatever was left of my greasy Arkansas gas station road-food into the toilet.

My mother, meanwhile, unaware of the Donner-tinged demise of the white mice, was now dreadfully worried about my health. I had apparently turned a sickly yellow color, and as I tearfully told her about the dead white mouse (I hadn't yet found the words to relay my dreadful conclusion about what happened to the "missing" one) my mother said, "Paul ... when's the last time you went to the bathroom?" Assuming she meant #1, I said, "At the gas station."

Delicately pressing the point a bit further, she asked, "And when was the last time you made #2?"

I said, "Before we left."

Pressing again, she asked, "Before we left Arkansas?"

By now, the conclusion of what this line of questioning was leading to was coming into view—and through tears, I wailed, "No. Before we left HOME."

As I write this story, I am once again struck by how insufficiently mothers are appreciated in our modern-day culture. Every one of 'em clearly deserves a medal—and my own mother should be first in the receiving line. But to return to my story.

In addition to the childhood traumas suffered on that Arkansas trip, there were also several pleasant takeaways—among them being my quickly-acquired taste for country ham, grits, and red-eye gravy; my discovery of that song "Alley Oop" on the jukebox of the local cafe; and a lifelong love for the songs of Jimmy Driftwood.

One song that still raises goosebumps for me is "St. Brendan's Fair Isle," which relates the story of Brendan the Navigator, an Irish priest and seafarer who was born in AD 484 and is primarily remembered for his legendary journey to the "Isle of the Blessed."

Setting out from Ireland with a crew of 16 like-minded monks in search of the Garden of Eden, the intrepid explorers experienced fantastic adventures on their seven-year voyage. In Driftwood's telling, these include confrontations with aquatic demons who burned sailors alive on the water and dragons who threatened to eat the entire crew. In each of the potential catastrophes, St. Brendan miraculously prevailed against the challenges, and the steadfastness of crew and leader was eventually rewarded by discovery of a miraculous land.

The plot thickens when they noticed their island appeared to be moving through the water—at which point St. Brendan explains that their new home is, in reality, the world's biggest fish. "Hold tight to the rope that's dragging our ship," he urges his courageous followers, as they'll need it someday, if the fish were to decide to take a plunge into the deep. As the song tells it, they sailed ten million miles in forty-four days on their fabulous journey. Not bad time by the standards of the 6th century, or, for that matter, the twenty-first.

James Morris was born in 1907. This is my salute to the writer of over 6,000 songs, an internationally known folklorist and performer, member of the Grand Ole Opry, advocate for environmental causes, poet laureate for trips big and small, and all-around exemplary human being—Jimmy Driftwood.

The Voyage of St. Brendan

Cardboard Boxes, and Origin Stories

Having parents (whether hetero or same–sex, biological or adopted) is a marvelous thing. If we didn't have them naturally, I suppose we'd have to invent them.

Of all the marvelous benefits we accrue from our parents, one that I've become particularly thankful for is those cardboard boxes they kept for decades up in the attic (or alternatively, down in the basement) within which our childhood mementos got diligently placed and stored. Thanks to their foresight, we can hop into a virtual time machine and view anew our childhood attempts at portraiture, crayola abstractions, and fledgling stabs at homegrown newspaper production (one of mine was called the "Chicago Sometimes"). Or, if one's parents were achievement-oriented, it's possible to reconnect with report cards from the fourth grade, marvel at which aptitudes we were then thought to possess, and take amusement from which skills were deemed insufficient.

In 1988, my mother, Millie, was planning a late-in-life move from New Haven, Connecticut to the Washington, DC area, in order to be closer to her grandchildren. As a result of that decision, she needed to winnow down the contents of the many cardboard boxes that she had dutifully kept for decades in her basement. Thorough planner that she was, she notified her kids six months in advance to make a trip to New Haven, so that each of us could rediscover and revive our childhood memories. And what a cache of memories we found in those boxes!

For example, it was something of a personal revelation to discover, from several of those report cards Mom kept, that my worst subject in those early years was penmanship. These days, in this era of word-processing, texting, and speech recognition software, penmanship is not as crucial a skill as it was once deemed to be. Especially cursive penmanship. Other than signing the occasional check, cursive handwriting has clearly become an obsolete skill, and one whose lack should represent no problem for most people in today's world. (Although OTHER people's difficulty with cursive handwriting later became a real problem for me, as I describe later in my piece "Killing the Blues" on the bizarre recording session of Norman Dayron).

Ironically enough, however, the discovery of my poor penmanship back in fourth grade provided some valuable insight 30 years later for analyzing and improving my right-hand skills on guitar. In particular, it helped me to find workarounds for my lifelong difficulty in mastering the machine-like plectrum technique of guitarists like John McLaughlin and Al DiMeola. A skill that, for me at least, is anything BUT obsolete.

Digging a bit deeper in the cardboard box, a few archeological strata below the report cards, and...*whoa*! What's THIS treasure trove? A bunch of black and white photos, clearly from the '50s, showing a bunch of school kids lined up in rows on makeshift bleachers. What are THESE all doing here? Who ARE these kids? And what's THIS one, with that one little white kid with the suspenders, second from the right, one row from the back?

It didn't take long to figure out that this was a photograph of my kindergarten class at Bousfield School, located at 45th and Drexel in an area known as Bronzeville, on Chicago's South Side. And it didn't take much longer for me to recognize that kid with the suspenders. I still occasionally do that little nervous tic of biting the inside of my cheek today.

As many friends have remarked in recent years, upon seeing the photo, "Wow, Paul. It wasn't too hard to figure out which one you were."

Bousfield School, Chicago, Illinois

And, of course, they're right. In the photo of me and those 36 other kindergarteners, it certainly isn't difficult to pick me out.

★ ★ ★ ★

Another fascinating discovery occurred 15 years later when my father Bernie died and my siblings and I gathered at his home in State College, PA to make crucial decisions concerning the arranging of his affairs. One of the many tasks ahead of us was to look through the dozens of cardboard boxes of mementos he had accumulated over the course of his life, and then decide who would be the most appropriate sibling to inherit each item of memorabilia. Much of what we found had to do with his career as a writer, and dozens of boxes of stuff relating to his long career were eventually donated to university libraries. But amidst the manuscripts, query sheets, and book reviews—the legacy of a lifetime as a professional author—were some fascinating tidbits that spoke of other milestones within his life.

In particular, one typewritten sheet, dated Dec 29, 1946 and considerably yellowed after 55 years, was hugely evocative for me. It was a semi-official letter of intent to engage the services of my dad and my mom, and hopefully persuade them to move from New York to Chicago in order to open a chapter of People's Songs there.

Amid the discussion about acquisition of essential furniture, donation of office supplies, and suggested compensation for my parents' roles in the organization, was a proposal concerning a fundraising concert to be held in Chicago. One sentence that jumped off the page, and still sticks in my memory to this day, was this one ...

"Of course, we hope Bernie will agree to play. Seeger has also indicated he'd be willing to be part of the concert. And we are hoping that Broonzy will agree to it as well, although he apparently wants $500 to do it, and that will make it very difficult to raise the money we need from this event."

As I time-traveled back 55 years and read this letter, it felt like someone had strummed a rich but complex chord on a guitar, with each string resonating deeply within the body of my own personal life.

To begin with: if my parents hadn't accepted the job offer, I would probably never have been born in Chicago. And therefore, never would have had ready access to a world inhabited by older blues musicians, all of whom had come there in the '30s and '40s as part of the "great migration" north from Mississippi, Arkansas, Louisiana, and surrounding southern states.

And had my dad not made his living for several years as a performing musician himself—and not had a guitar around the house, long after he acquired another calling in life—I might not have gravitated towards a fascination with the instrument at an early age.

And had I not occasionally been bounced on Big Bill Broonzy's knee in my parents' home as a toddler, I might not have been drawn so powerfully to the music that he and many of his fellow blues musicians played—music whose language I had an opportunity to absorb into my own, and eventually used to build a career as a professional musician myself.

I then reflected on the awkwardness posed by Bill's high-dollar quote for his services. Certainly, everyone involved in the People's Songs organization must have felt uncomfortable entering into a hardball fee negotiation with a Black man whose career and livelihood they wished to support. But serving as counterweight to that discomfort, one presumes, was the obvious fact that a fundraiser can't succeed if the lion's share of proceeds wind up going to one high-profile performer—a performer who understandably might be viewing the fundraiser as "just another gig." As a professional musician myself—one who's played a lifetime of benefit shows while simultaneously attempting to earn a living—I've felt and been on both sides of that emotionally fraught issue.

Reflecting further on my parents' choice to move to Chicago in 1946, I considered where in that sprawling city they chose to live and raise a family. Their choice to live on the South Side was one clearly made in congruence with the world-view of friends like Pete Seeger and the People's Songs cohort, whose values included living in what sociology-minded folks now call a "culturally diverse world." Had my parents chosen differently, I certainly wouldn't have attended Bousfield School in Bronzeville, and might never have grown up surrounded by faces whose color was much darker than mine.

Would growing up in another neighborhood really have made a difference in my life, my values, and my attitudes towards my fellow man? After all, conventional wisdom holds that we inherit most of our core values from our parents. So, given that, how much would it really have mattered what color my neighbors and classmates were, in terms of how I turned out 75 years later?

I was discussing this very question with a friend when I started to reminiscence about the summer of 1959, when I was attending the 53rd Street YMCA, located just a few blocks from my house.

During those hot summer days, all us neighborhood kids would enthusiastically pile into a big yellow school bus, waiting to take us out of the sweltering city for a few hours. Then, after a half-hour drive to a forest preserve west of the city, we'd all noisily pile out of the bus, run around in the relatively green wooded area to blow off some youthful steam, find a bit of mischief to get into, and finally head back to the city and the Y.

Then, at the point when the bus pulled within a block or two of the Y, and familiar neighborhood landmarks became recognizable through the open windows, all the kids would excitedly start chanting, "Chocolate

dip! Chocolate dip!" Which we all knew meant a jump in the pool for a quick swim to freshen up after the sweaty afternoon's activities.

At this point in my reminiscence, my friend interrupted to say, "Wow. Sounds like a fun memory. But how come they were yelling 'chocolate dip?'"

I explained that we were all really hot and sticky after the forest preserve hijinks, since summers in Chicago can get awfully brutal. And buses at that time didn't have air-conditioning.

She said, "Yeah, I get all that. But why CHOCOLATE dip?"

At first, I didn't understand the question. It all seemed so obvious. It's just what excited kids do after a hot and sweaty afternoon. Right?

Then, it hit me.

As the anecdote makes clear, I never considered back then what in retrospect appears obvious. Namely, that most of my friends—whether in school, in Little League, or at the Y—were Black. The moral, I guess, is that it's remarkable what kids can be blissfully unaware of when they're "just being kids."

But IS that really the moral? After all, kids are blissfully unaware of a LOT of things. Things that eventually take on a great deal of importance, as one hops into that virtual time machine and reflects on one's life from a distance.

So, again. How much would it really have mattered what color my neighbors and classmates were while I was growing up, in terms of how I turned out 75 years later?

Hard to say. But here's my best guess.

My feeling is that growing up as a minority within society—as opposed to being in the MAJORITY culture of that society—is a huge formative factor in how you eventually perceive yourself and the world around you. Growing up as a minority makes you do a bit more thinking before speaking, and a bit more second-guessing of yourself before acting. Less inclined towards overconfidence and hubris, and more inclined to question the likelihood of success. More likely to look both ways before running out in the street … and less likely to assume that your way IS, in fact, the highway.

And, I might add, I believe this to be true whether the child is Black growing up in a white world, or whether the child is white growing up in a Black one.

★ ★ ★ ★

While engaged in the process of compiling these essays into the book that you're now reading, I showed some of them to a writer friend in hopes of soliciting his advice and wisdom. After reading them, he said something that stuck with me.

"There's a unique and interesting blend of music anecdotes and origin stories here, Paul." Needless to say, I appreciated the kind words. But that wasn't the part that stuck with me.

What stuck with me was the term "origin story."

My friend's comment took me back to the very first time I heard the term "origin story." It was in a History of Comparative Religions class that I had taken at the University of Chicago, where I was first introduced to the writings of a man named Mircea Eliade. Eliade's contention was that every culture develops a cosmology—an origin story—in order to explain how the universe was originally created, and how humans came to be part of it. And further to his point, he proposed that human beings require the myths and stories they have created as a way to make sense of their lives—in the larger spiritual sense, but also in the sense of an individual's personal journey through life.

But my writer friend was clearly not referencing religion classes, sacred texts and spiritual journeys, or astrophysical explanations for the universe when he was describing my essays. As I quickly realized, he was referencing an apparently more modern under-standing of the term "origin stories"—that is, the backstories and events that a fiction author creates to explain why a character develops in the way that they did, and how they got to be who they eventually become.

So, how did a term clearly used by anthropologists and Divinity School professors morph into a term now associated with Hollywood screenwriting? My curiosity now piqued, I looked into the riddle. And what I found connected me right back to those cardboard boxes.

The answer to the riddle, as near as I can figure, is writer Stan Lee and his fabulous creations, which he marketed as "Marvel Comics." As it happens, I myself was an avid devourer of Marvel Comics during the early '60s when I was a teen, and I vividly recall taking delight in the science-fiction-inspired world Lee constructed episode by episode around his characters. In each of his comics, Lee created an elaborate "backstory" for his superheroes, thus providing an additional layer of dramatic complexity to what otherwise would have come across as simplistic, childish fantasy.

So now, jumping into that virtual time machine and setting it forward 55 years, I discover that the term "origin story" used by my writer friend has become universally recognized shorthand within the literary community when referring to that now-ubiquitous convention. Although originally associated with Stan Lee, the phrase is now routinely tossed around in studio boardrooms whenever blockbuster movies and big-budget television dramas are discussed.

Learning of the connection between Stan Lee's comics and the writers' world that I was beginning to dip my toe into was fascinating. And, additionally, made me wonder whatever happened to those piles of Marvel Comics I was so crazy about collecting as a teen.

Well, much to my chagrin, the stacks and stacks of Spiderman, Fantastic Four, and Silver Surfer comics that I passionately collected as a kid were NOT found in those cardboard boxes in the basement. I suspect my mom spent less than 30 seconds mulling it before deciding to throw the whole batch of them in the trash. Too bad, because those comics I was so fond of back in the '60s are now highly collectible—and bundled together, they would now be worth a small fortune. Had mom thought to save those comics, along with my report cards and kindergarten photos, I could probably retire comfortably on the proceeds.

Evidently though, my mom had her own metrics for what she imagined her son would value decades later. And understandably, I suppose, the peculiarities and quirks of a collectibles market, 50 years in the future, were simply not on her radar screen. After all, how COULD they be? Who could have predicted the nostalgic eccentricities that motivate baby-boomers nowadays to spend absurd sums in an effort to revisit and reclaim their childhood fetishes?

Well, maybe SOMEONE could have. But not my mom.

It's often been noted that in our language, the word "value" works a double shift—

serving as a unit of measure for how many dollars a widget costs, and also serving to denote the deeply rooted moral codes that each of us live by. Odd that the same word could have such seemingly disparate meanings in our language and culture…no?

Odd or no, it certainly could be argued that the choice of which denotation of "value" one chooses to go through life using says a great deal about the person doing the choosing.

Are you a person who reflexively sees life through the lens of the material, monetary worth of things?

Or are you a person who finds life's value in the wellbeing of those around them, and finds satisfaction in living according to your ethical and moral codes?

My parents have been gone for decades now. I often wish I could haul out that time machine, travel back 50 years, and talk to my parents concerning the choices they made in their lives. If I did, I'd tell them the very same thing my friends said when they first looked at my kindergarten picture:

"Mom and Dad, it wasn't too hard to figure out which one you were."

★ ★ ★ ★

Backing out of that time machine setting, and resetting the dial back to the present day (whoosh!) it's not especially surprising that my parents' four acorns didn't fall far from the tree.

Now, in thinking about these mementos that my mom and dad thoughtfully saved from decades earlier, I can see how those report cards, kindergarten photos, and letters they kept in those cardboard boxes in the attic served as personal Rosetta Stones for my own origin story. Each one of those mementos represents a valuable clue for deciphering why I developed in the way that I did, and how I got to be who I've eventually become.

At the risk of repeating myself, having parents is a marvelous thing. A thing that, unlike a time machine, we DON'T have to invent.

And speaking of marvelous inventions—whoever invented the cardboard box certainly deserves a round of applause. If it were up to me, I'd call them up onstage and give them a medal.

Café Au Go Go street scene

"Is It A Blues Record?"

The summer of 1966 often found me attending blues shows at a NYC club called the Café Au Go Go, on Bleecker Street. Performers I saw that summer included Junior Wells, John Lee Hooker, and the Butterfield Blues Band, each leaving a deep impression.

The Beatles had already captured the hearts of most of my friends, and they had just released a record called *Rubber Soul*, which had begun to win me over as well. But my deepest affection was still for the bluesmen who I had been listening to since my early teens.

One day, my friend and music companion Peter Blum suggested we go to a show featuring the singer John Hammond. I had seen Hammond several times already and was reluctant to spend what little money I had seeing him again—but Peter insisted, pointing out that this show would be different. THIS show had him fronting an electric blues band—and Peter made a big point of the lead guitarist, who he described as amazing and not to be missed.

Well, Peter was right. This guy was effortlessly capable of channeling the very best of my then-favorite players like Buddy Guy, Otis Rush, and Elmore James, while taking the familiar vocabulary of licks and tones even further. I was totally transfixed by the playing and stage presence of this guy ... whose name, apparently, was Jimmy James.

But life went on, and I soon found other music to be enthralled by. And over time, the memory of that show receded.

Fast forward to the next summer, when my friend Peter called me and asked if I was in town. Actually, I was, since I was living in NYC that summer, and he said that

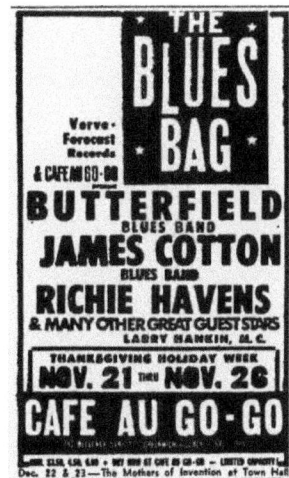

he had just bought a record that he thought I'd want to hear. My curiosity piqued, I asked whose record it was. He said, "Well, you remember when we went to hear John Hammond? And you remember the guitarist he had with him? Well, he's now got a record out, under his own name."

I said, "Cool. I'd love to hear it. Is it a blues record?" Peter said "Uh … not exactly. But it's pretty incredible. The record's called *Are You Experienced?* And he added, "I just bought some stereo headphones, and you really need to listen to it on them."

"Oh," he said. "And it turns out Jimmy James isn't really his name. His real name is Jimi Hendrix."

Jimi passed away in 1970, a few months shy of his 28th birthday. Rock on, Jimi, on whatever planet you are now playing. You were certainly one of the most inspiring and influential electric guitarists on THIS one.

Jimi Hendrix

MIDDLEBURY COLLEGE BULLETIN

MIDDLEBURY, VERMONT
APRIL 1946

Bread Loaf

WRITERS'
CONFERENCE

Leonard Cohen, Bob Dylan, and Finding Our Way Home

By the mid-'50s, my dad was well on his way out of one life's calling and into another.

As his father-in-law had predicted, a career built around writing and performing socially progressive songs for political rallies and labor union meetings wasn't bringing in enough income to support a wife and two kids—especially with another one shortly on the way. Being blacklisted in Red Channels certainly didn't help matters, either—so when opportunities presented themselves to write liner notes for LPs, reviews for music trade publications, or churn out promo copy for local jazz clubs, my dad eagerly took each assignment, resolving to use them to sharpen his skills and develop his craft.

In 1958, dad took a major plunge. With his wife and oldest child (me) in tow, he drove 1,000 miles east from Chicago to the tiny town of Ripton, Vermont to attend a ten-day-long writers' workshop called The Bread Loaf Writers' Conference—a place that was thought of as a "rite of passage" for one hoping to parlay their literary calling into a professional career.

As a child of nine, my own recollections of the event are fuzzy and frustratingly shallow. If I was sufficiently convinced of the efficacy of hypnosis to unlock childhood memories, I would seriously consider employing it to revisit that time and discover how our stay in Bread Loaf shaped my later life. I suspect the answer might turn out to be, "not much."

But I DO know what those ten days meant to my dad.

For many years afterwards, my dad would refer to Bread Loaf as the place where he first experienced why he was put on earth, and what he was meant to do here. His true calling, he discovered, was to write.

And write, he did. And not just promo copy and music reviews, but articles for respected magazines. And shortly thereafter—books. MANY books, on many topics, over the 40 years that followed.

A few months back, I returned from a visit to Bread Loaf myself, where I was hired to present two classes—one devoted to the songs of Bob Dylan, and the other on those of Leonard Cohen.

The Dylan class was arguably one I've been unwittingly preparing for all my life, since the time exactly 60 years ago when I attended a Pete Seeger concert with my dad, and went backstage to get the autograph of the young songwriter who had just torn the top of my head off, poured a mixture of hydrochloric acid and LSD into it, and set it ablaze.

But the Leonard Cohen assignment was a bit more of a stretch. Not having ever been a deep fan of the Canadian songwriter, I needed to do some homework in order to pull it off. Fortunately, however, I'm married to a woman who is probably Leonard's biggest fan on the planet—so between the two of us, we were able to present five of his tunes in dramatic and musically artful ways.

One of the most interesting aspects of the class was a deep dive into the religious imagery within the songs—some obvious, some only evident to theologically-trained minds. Of which there were many in the class—including my wife Celia, who teaches theology classes at Loyola.

Before leaving the Bread Loaf campus, we drove across the road to visit the spot where—at his request 22 years ago—I spread the contents of an urn containing my dad's ashes. Dad wanted what was left of him to be in the place where he found his true calling.

Whenever Dad would visit me in Vermont, he would invariably say, "Let's go grab breakfast, and then drive someplace in this beautiful state of yours." I would say, "Where do you have in mind?" and he would invariably say, "Oh, I don't know. Let's just take a drive and see where we wind up."

Of course, after the third or fourth time he visited, I KNEW what he had in mind—and where we would wind up. An hour or so into the drive, Dad would say, "Hey! Where are we, relative to the town of Hancock? Or Ripton? Do you think we could figure out a way to drive there, on our way home?"

Of course, we can, Dad. I'm sure we can find a way to wind up at Bread Loaf. And from there, find our way home.

A Steel Guitar Whines Low

My dad was never one to shy away from an argument when an important point needed to be made. Even when he ran the risk of jeopardizing his professional career.

Once during the early '60s, a group of notable, respected writers were in our living room, discussing the ins and outs of their craft. Although I was in another room in the house, I couldn't help but overhear my dad expounding on a topic that I knew to be near and dear to his heart—the necessity for a writer to express their point as simply and as directly as possible.

As he spoke, the volume in the room began to rise, and the voices of my dad's writer friends became increasingly strident. I crept over to a spot near the door to hear what all the fuss was about—and became somewhat alarmed, as I realized that many of his colleagues appeared to be ridiculing my dad. Though I was just a kid, I was already aware by then that my dad was relatively new to his profession—and I knew that he needed the support and respect of these older, more experienced men and women to succeed.

At that moment, my dad got up, walked towards the hi-fi in the corner of the room and said "I want to play you an example of what I'm talking about." For a moment, the room fell silent—and then, the whine of a steel guitar filled the room. There were a few nervous, uncomfortable giggles. And then, in a voice slathered over with Alabama twang, the singer began to sing the song that my dad intended as the object lesson for his colleagues.

Hank Williams

The song he chose to play was "I'm So Lonesome I Could Cry", written and recorded in my birth year of 1949 by country music icon Hank Williams.

The plaintive tone of a lonesome whippoorwill filled the room, as the singer delivered the spare poetry of the first verse in a Jimmie Rodgers-inspired timbre rarely heard above the Mason-Dixon line. As lyrical clouds began to cover the face of the now-weeping moon, quizzical looks of confusion and disbelief began to appear on the faces of my dad's friends.

The confusion deepened as Jerry Byrd's Rickenbacker steel guitar reprised the low whine of the midnight train which had had made its atmospheric entrance and exit in the first verse. And shortly afterwards, the weeping of a robin, bemoaning the dying leaves at summer's end, emerged from the speakers of our family's Hi-Fi.

By now, the confusion of my dad's friends had coalesced into a consensus, and the giggles had turned to outright laughter. "Bernie. What IS this?" one guest hooted. Another friend said in a derisive tone, "It's like a Hallmark card. 'When you care to sing the very best.'" Everyone in the room roared.

My dad stood his ground. "You're all missing this. THIS is great American story-telling. I don't understand how you can't see that." To say the moment was an awkward one would be an understatement.

Well, I can't say that my dad was right on the money with EVERY point he espoused over the years. But he certainly got THAT one right.

Over the last 50 years—thanks to a healthy populist strain on the rise in American culture—the literary and intellectual world has managed to pull its head out of its own collective ass, and has come around to seeing his point.

Hiram Williams was born on September 17, 1923. The all-time great songwriter and irreplaceable icon of country music died in the back seat of a car driving to a New Years' Day show in Canton, Ohio. He was 29 years old.

Duxbury, VT 1971

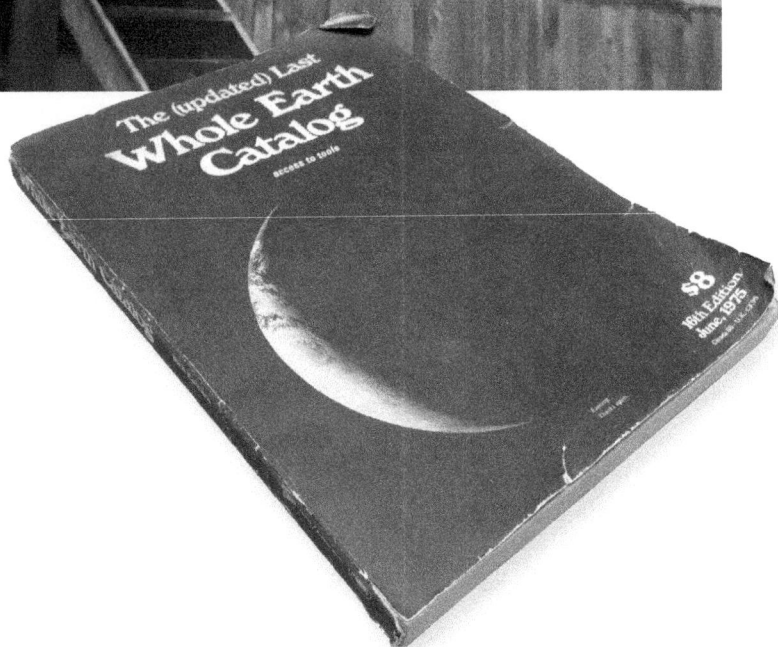

Big Mama Thornton and Her Hound Dog Cadenza

In May 1972, I observed the anniversary of my first year in my newly adopted home of North Duxbury, Vermont.

Somehow, the Geodesic Dome that my girlfriend and I had planned for months using *The Whole Earth Catalog* had actually gotten built on our 6.3 acres of rugged mountain terrain. Even more miraculously, both hands—and all ten fingers—had somehow survived the experience intact and unscathed.

As a native Chicagoan, I was inured to tough winters. And that first Vermont winter certainly didn't disappoint in that regard. The dome and its two inhabitants may have managed to survive the challenges of heavy snow loads, freezing pipes, and impassible roads—but after a year of isolated rural life, I began to understand the phenomenon that my neighbors referred to as "cabin fever." My previous life of six-night-a-week gigging in Chicago blues clubs hadn't prepared me for the "cold turkey detox" of my new lifestyle, and the isolated rural environment I had chosen a year earlier.

It was at that point that I received a phone call from a friend in Plainfield, asking whether I wanted to be part of a hastily-assembled backup band for a blues veteran named Willie Mae "Big Mama" Thornton. Big Mama was not especially well-known to the world at large. But in 1952 she recorded a song named "Hound Dog," written by two white guys named Jerry Lieber and Mike Stoller, which would skyrocket another not-especially-well-known white singer named Elvis Presley to stardom.

I had previously only seen Willie Mae once before, but had played with many "one-degree-of-separation" musicians who knew her well.

Their stories were vivid—and made abundantly clear that the cantankerous, supremely self-possessed voice heard on that iconic song in '52 was not just a vocal affectation.

And so it was that 20 years later, I found myself setting up my Fender Deluxe Reverb amplifier on the stage of an auditorium called the HayBarn, on the campus of the legendarily counter-culture institution, Goddard College. Along with me were a group of musicians who I had just met—many of whom I remain friends with to this day.

As is customary in the blues world, the band played several tunes to warm up the audience. At that point, the tried-and-true blues script would require that one of the band members step up to the microphone and initiate a vocal introduction for the headliner of the evening—"Ladies and gentlemen … it's with great pleasure that I present to you the star of our show … an artist who first hit with "You Ain't Nuthin' But a Hound Dog … " who's sung the blues from Houston, Texas to San Francisco, California to Great Britain … and is now here in beautiful Plainfield, Vermont to sing for you all … the woman you've all been waiting for … Ms. BIG MAMA THORNTON!"

And at that point, the by-now deliriously excited crowd would begin a gradually escalating, rhythmic chant of her name, as she slowly sashayed from behind the curtain, took the stage, walked up to the mic, thanked her audience, and with a brief nod to the band, began her first song.

Well … none of that actually happened.

What, in fact, actually happened is that Mama wandered out on stage approximately halfway into the band's third song, slowly picking her way through the maze of instruments cluttering the floor while we played. She then stood in front of the mic, staring out at the audience of raggedly dressed, largely unshaven, and likely unwashed hippies. A look of bewilderment was unmistakable on her face as the band limped through the last 30 seconds of what clearly would be our last instrumental warm-up tune.

Casting her eye over the audience of kids littering the floor, Mama's eyes settled on one young man lying on the floor, his head in his girlfriend's lap, casually sucking her thumb. Mama watched him as he occasionally removed her thumb to holler enthusiastically, before returning the girlfriend's thumb to his mouth. She slowly shook her head in disbelief, then turned around and muttered to no one in particular before launching into her first tune of the evening.

Given the fact that the band had never rehearsed together, the first couple of songs came off surprisingly well. But eventually, the juxtaposition of cultures reared its comically ugly head.

For our third tune, Big Mama counted off her signature song "Ball and Chain"—a tune which was first introduced to white audiences after it became a hit and a staple of Janis Joplin's repertoire. Things were going relatively well, and the song was building to its dramatic climax, when a large German shepherd wandered out from the wings and onto the stage. Laughter and hoots of appreciation broke out in the audience. Sensing that the hoots and hollers were not in sync with the drama of the song, Willie May looked around, and saw the dog slowly but surely making its way to center stage.

At this point, her disbelief at the ridiculousness of the entire situation morphed into anger. She signaled emphatically with her hand—which our drummer initially interpreted as signals for a rimshot for lyrical emphasis.

But no. It quickly became clear that her emphatic signals were NOT intended for lyrical emphasis. They were intended to bring the music to a halt. And bring it to a halt we did.

To the suddenly silent room, the star of our show … the artist who'd come all the way from Houston, Texas to sing the blues… the woman we'd all been waiting for … proceeded to deliver a ten-minute-long, *a capella*, totally impromptu speech to the stunned audience of dazed hippies on the impossible rudeness of allowing a dog to wander on-stage for her performance.

And then, when she had expressed every ounce of her indignation and righteous fury—fueled in no small part by a lifetime of being ignored by a music industry more interested in short-term profit than in supporting the artists who actually created the music—she suddenly kicked into the dramatic vocal cadenza: "Why love is like … why love is like … why love is like, a ball and … CHAIN." At which point, the band kicked into the time-honored traditional blues ending, and the audience broke into ecstatic applause.

As I write this, over 50 years later, I'm trying to imagine how this same scenario could possibly have occurred in a Chicago blues club. Or a concert. Or a blues festival. Of course, I can't. It would never have happened.

But, here in my newly-adopted home of rural Vermont, at a hippie college enclave, it was hardly unimaginable. Or shocking. I had, in fact, come to take things like a dog wandering onto the stage in the middle of a show without a bit of surprise. Or shock.

I s'pose it goes to show what a year in the country—and a heavy dose of cabin fever—can do to your head.

Willie Mae Thornton was born on Dec 11, 1926. She passed away in 1984, and was buried in a pauper's grave. The world remembers her as the woman whose song "Hound Dog" made a world-renowned, national icon out of a young kid from Tupelo, MS—the one-of-a-kind Big Mama Thornton.

Big Mama Thornton

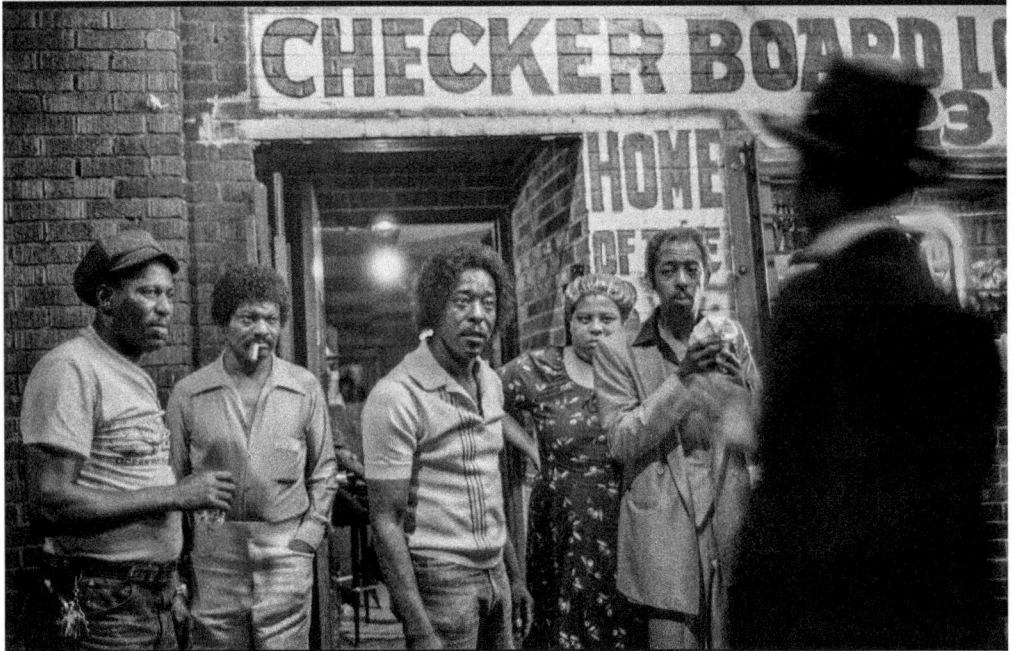

Buddy Guy, Lefty Dizz and others, Checkerboard Lounge

Bill Berg, and His '52 Goldtop

Getting old has its drawbacks—but I'm told it beats the alternative. Plus, there are some lovely benefits to having friends you've known for 55 years.

Bill Berg and I have known each other from our South Side Chicago days, in the late '60s. I was working small clubs on the South and West Side, getting a minor reputation as the new white boy on the scene who could actually play the stuff right. Meanwhile, Bill, a few years older than me, had already befriended many of my employers, and his med-school training enabled him to provide medical care and advice to some of these guys, who often had scant options in that regard.

Over the years, we kept in touch—through our moves to the East Coast, and through our various marital and professional changes. Much in our lives had changed—but at some point in our evenings together, the conversation would inevitably turn to the old days.

At that point, the many epic tall tales we collectively had accumulated over the years would get ceremoniously trotted out—scary shootouts in clubs, sudden flareups and tense situations on the street outside, harrowing experiences in unfamiliar cities while on the road, and the dozens of unsubstantiated but racy rumors concerning mutual musician acquaintances we had known. With each retelling, the stories inevitably took on slightly new embellishments and wrinkles for our own amusement and amazement.

Our wives, Melinda and Celia, would roll their eyes, and as our scuttle-butting grew more vivid, they would decamp to another corner of the room—presumably to engage in conversations more becoming of intelligent human beings.

Bill Berg's '52 Les Paul Goldtop

A few years ago, Bill told me of his desire to bequeath to me his old guitar from the South Side days. Not just ANY guitar, but his old '52 Les Paul Goldtop.

Now, guitar geeks will instantly recognize that a '52 Les Paul Goldtop is close to the top of the pantheon of iconic, collectible guitar models. Pristine, unmodified, and well-cared-for examples are lusted after due to their rarity, and have become extremely valuable in the last few decades.

(These days, ownership of valuable guitars has become the exclusive province of hedge fund managers, dentists, and aging rock stars—not musicians who made them iconic through actually playing them. But that's another story, for another time.)

However, THIS '52 Les Paul Goldtop was hardly pristine, unmodified, or well-cared-for. In the parlance of collectors, Bill's guitar had been woefully "boogered." Much of the boogery had taken place before Bill ever owned it. But the fact is that over the years, many of us—myself definitely included—have committed what in retrospect seem like mortal sins to our now-collectible guitars.

During the late '60s, instruments were considered simply tools to make the meager living their music afforded their owners. The idea of being reluctant to diminish the value of what might once become a valuable collectible was the furthest thing from our minds. But that, too, is another story for another day.

I still vividly remember the afternoon when FedEx delivered the box containing Bill Berg's old, hardly pristine, hugely modified, not especially well-cared-for '52 Les Paul Goldtop. Now, sitting here, looking at its completely decaled, '60s-ed-out case, I can't help but reflect on all the painful, bizarre, and occasionally beautiful aspects of this thing we call "the aging process."

Inevitably, like guitars, our bodies and our friendships morph over time, acquiring odd scars, modifications, and patinas from use. But there are still songs left to sing, new arrangements to work out, and fresh solos to play.

Rock on Bill. And thanks for thinking of your old South Side buddy. I'll always treasure your guitar!

Maceo's New Suit

In late 1977, I started developing pain in my left-hand wrist, which gradually grew more pronounced as the weeks went on. As near as I could tell, it started when I bought a friend's bass and began using it while playing gigs with a jazz pianist. Although by then I had been a professional guitarist for over ten years, I was still fairly unversed in the dark art of instrument setup—that is, understanding how to adjust the instrument so as to get a good, clean, and buzz-free sound without pushing down with the left-hand fingers more than necessary.

As a result of playing this poorly set-up instrument, my left hand got extremely fatigued after a relatively short while; and after a few gigs—which I got through by gritting my teeth and trusting in the philosophy of "no pain, no gain"—I was forced to the realization that I had truly injured myself.

Up to the time of my injury, I had been playing quite a bit, and teaching a lot as well. But this all changed when it became clear that I could no longer play guitar for more than a minute or two without pain setting in. I saw doctors, PTs, and health professionals of all sorts over the next few months, but nothing seemed to work.

Eventually, in desperation, I took a long-shot suggestion from a friend and drove down to Middlebury to see a beekeeper named Charlie Mraz. Charlie was a proponent of something called "bee venom therapy," which had proved quite helpful for people with advanced cases of rheumatoid arthritis. The way the therapy worked was, the sufferer would carefully reach into a jar containing honey bees, extract one using long tweezers, and place it on the forearm until the bee responded by stinging. Once stung, the bee was discarded, and the process repeated several times each day.

The measure of my desperation was evidenced by the fact that I left Charlie's place with a large bell jar full of bees, and dutifully performed this ritual everyday for several months.

But to no avail. The pain refused to leave.

At some point, in the early days of my desperate search for a cure, a girlfriend of mine had suggested taking some time off "to do something for myself." "You know," she said, "something that you would never do if you were working all the time, but now have the freedom to do because you're NOT working." I had initially rejected the idea, because it seemed to me that the affliction couldn't last too much longer. But as the months passed, without any symptomatic improvement, the idea started making sense.

And that's how the plan for a "create your own adventure" road trip through the South was born.

After several weeks on the road, I finally reached the southernmost stop on my journey: New Orleans. A couple who I knew from Vermont were now living in the French Quarter, in a slightly rundown building just off Royal Street, that once was a slave quarters. (Buildings like these are now extremely attractive, spendy digs. But back then, before NOLA was "mainstream-ed" as a cool destination, they were cheap and easily available.) My friends happened to be out of town, but they generously offered me their place as base camp for my explorations. And explore I did.

Of course, there were music clubs—from funky hole-in-the-walls like Benny's Bar (and whatever bar that was in the Quarter where me and three other patrons watched James Booker play for hours) to more iconic (but just as funky) spots like Rosy's, Jimmy's and Tipitina's. And of course, there were restaurants—though I could only afford to patronize small neighborhood joints like Buster Holmes, The Hummingbird Grill, and as a splurge, Austin Leslie's wonderful Chez Helene.

And then, there were the junk-tique shops that were scattered along Decatur Street … and at one of these shops, I saw my first Mardi Gras Indian costume. Although, at the time, I had no idea what it was—and therefore assumed what I was seeing was a unique, one-of-a-kind creation made by a Liberace wannabe on a psilocybin trip. Until I saw another. And then, another. And another. And slowly began to realize this was a THING. One that—like so many other things down there—seemed to be unique to New Orleans culture. Specifically, New Orleans BLACK culture.

Allison "Tootie" Montana, Big Chief of the Yellow Pocahontas

Of course, if you grew up in New Orleans, you'd know all about Mardi Gras—the floats, the Krewes, the second line parades, and the Mardi Gras Indians. And presumably, you'd know something about the hundreds of hours that go into making each year's unique costume. So in 1975, when a new song by the Mardi Gras Indian tribe The Wild Magnolias comes on the radio with the lyric "Every year, at carnival time, we make a new suit"—well, you'd know exactly what the hell the singer was singing about.

But to a kid from Chicago, the concept was an entirely mind-blowing one.

Eventually, the pain in my wrist subsided. And not long after returning home from my trip, I began playing with a small group of musicians that ultimately coalesced as Kilimanjaro. Once I resumed playing, and began writing music for the group, my seven months of musical down-time were quickly forgotten. But the irresistibly funky rhythmic groove of the Magnolias' carnival staple "New Suit" stuck in my mind for decades—until it eventually wound up serving as inspiration for the tune "Maceo's New Suit" on Kilimanjaro's 2009 CD, *Homecoming*.

I often think of that 1978 trip to New Orleans, and the countless number of pilgrimages I've made since then. As anyone who visits the city can attest, something about the place and its people stays with you, even when you're no longer there. This is especially true for those of us who make music that draws on the city's rich and deep culture.

As Crescent City R&B great Ernie K-Doe once said, "I'm not sure, but I'm almost positive, that all music came from New Orleans." Once the spirit of the place makes its way inside you after a few weeks there, any exaggeration that your skeptical mind might be inclined to detect in that attribution falls away—replaced by an abiding acceptance that every irresistibly funky rhythm within American dance music, every sonority of every brass band, and every improvised vocal line within a popular song, must have originally come from this city and its culture.

I'm sure that there are people who have derived a great deal of benefit from their ritual inoculation of venom from Charlie Mraz's bees. I just happened not to be one of them. But the regular administration of Crescent City culture into my musical life has been a continuous source of inspiration ever since that first visit. And based on its overall efficacy, and the long-lasting effects when taken as a regular regimen, I can't imagine why I'd want to stop now.

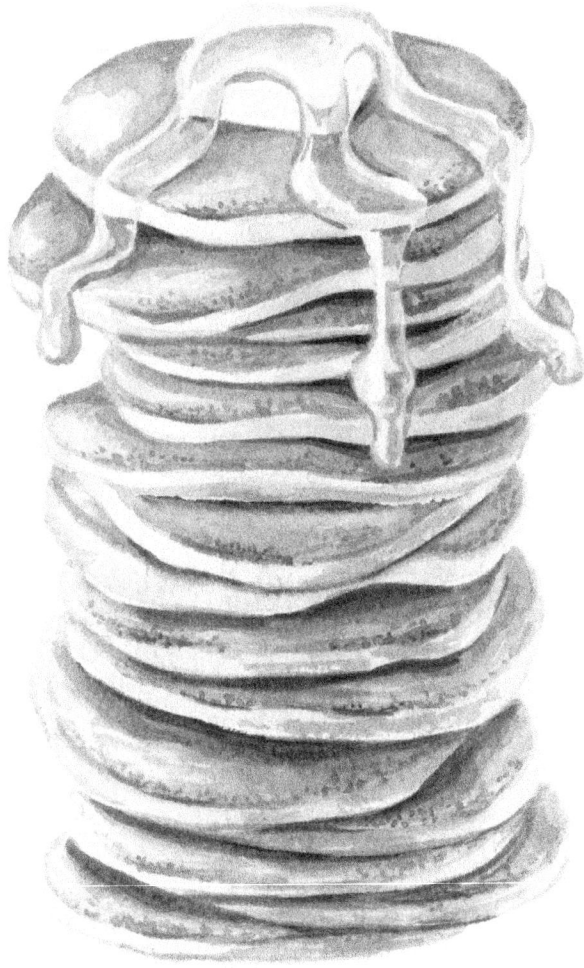

Woke Up This Morning

I never fail to to be impressed by what a savvy, aware, and tuned-in bunch of friends I am fortunate to have in my life. (I won't say "Woke," now that a certain faction of our political class has publicly demonized the use of that otherwise wholly unobjectionable term. So, I'll just stick with my three previous descriptors). Therefore, I'm sure I hardly need to point out the obvious fact that today, February 28, is quite a special day.

Sorry, no—I wasn't referring to "National Pancake Day" (Yes, that's actually a thing. I assume that's an annual observance that IHOP's lobbyists insisted on, in return for their campaign contributions to their reliably cooperative carbohydrate-consuming congressional candidates.)

And again, sorry but no. I wasn't referring to "National Chocolate Souffle Day" either (which is ALSO a thing, though I can certainly see why you'd confuse the two events. However, I suspect that IHOP was NOT behind this particular February 28 remembrance. Possibly, this was some GOP senators' invention after their 2003 "Freedom Fries" protest made the US something of a laughingstock—and therefore, they felt it necessary to extend a conciliatory gesture to long-time US ally and inventors of universally-recognized gourmet confections, the French?)

Anyway, the special event that I'm referring to—which we as a nation apparently celebrate each year—is "National Public Sleeping Day." Yes, you know the one—the day that "was founded with the purpose of encouraging people to be sure they get enough sleep."

And no, I'm NOT making this up. It's ALL easily found on the website "daysoftheyear.com"—which I encourage one and all to visit, read, and be amazed by.

And when you go there yourself, you'll be asked to "Consider all of the times it's been a delight to see someone else have a bit of a nap in public, whether on a bus or in the waiting room of a medical office." Which, presumably, brings to mind delightfully warm and fuzzy personal recollections for each of us.

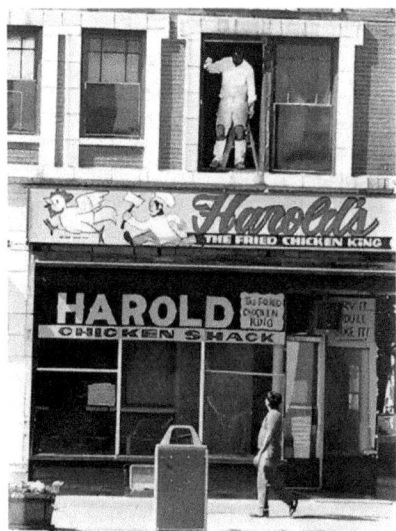

Harold's Chicken Shack, 53rd St, Chicago

For me personally, it brings to mind the apartment I rented for several years on 53rd Street in Chicago, right above Harold's Chicken Shack—and the delight I felt each morning while carefully stepping over the wino who slept in the vestibule at the foot of the stairs.

Believe it or not, I later found that our former president Barack Obama lived in that very same apartment building, directly over Harold's Chicken Shack.

How do I know that?

Well, I found out that tantalizing tidbit directly from the horse's mouth, so to speak, when newly-minted FLOTUS Michelle Obama was being interviewed on *60 Minutes* in November 2008. At one point, while reminiscing about Barack's first apartment in DC, and his notoriously frugal lifestyle, Michelle compared it to the Chicago apartment he lived in "when we first started dating."

Recalling the memory, Barack nodded his head, chuckled, and said, "Yeah. The one right over Harold's Chicken Shack."

Needless to say, my head exploded on the spot. Hearing that the President of the United States and I may have shared the same crib, twenty years apart, was something I could never imagined happening in this lifetime.

Anyway, the delight I get from the memory of the wino who slept in the vestibule at the foot of the stairs is enhanced every time I reflect on the UC-law-professor-turned-US-senator-turned-POTUS gingerly stepping over that same fellow. Or perhaps, stepping over another, different-but-equally-proud standard-bearer who was also taking the opportunity to celebrate the National Public Sleeping Day tradition—since Barack would have lived in that apartment building with Michelle a good twenty plus years after I did.

But again, I digress …

The point I'm trying to make here is that sleeping anywhere—whether in public, or in your own bed—is indeed a delightful thing. But it's made all the more delightful when you eventually wake up—whether in the morning, or the crack o' noon, as many of my musician colleagues prefer. Perhaps we need to reflect on the larger truth that—much like the ears that, by HEARING the falling tree, actually CREATE the sound in Descartes' philosophical forest—it's the actual WAKING UP that makes the sleeping delightful.

Hopefully we can all agree on that? I mean, imagine if you were asleep, but didn't ever actually … Well, I think you get the idea.

The Unknown Blues Band at Discover Jazz Festival

Anyway, this is what I believe the Port Huron Pressure Cooker … the King of the Buzzard Strut … the one and only … (drum roll, please!) … Big Joe Burrell was getting at in the song "Woke Up This Morning," which the Unknown Blues Band recorded in 1981, and which can be found on our *Live At Hunt's* CD.

This tune was one of our favorites back in the days when saxophones were mellow, dinosaurs walked the earth, phish swam in the sea, and The Unknown Blues Band ruled the forest of Burlington, Vermont's nightlife.

If you remember those days … well, then, you know.

The Unknown Blues Band with Big Joe Burrell, Red Square, Moscow, Russia

Flame-Broiled Shashlik, Eli Whitney, and Kilimanjaro's Russian Tour

In November of 1991, my band Kilimanjaro toured Russia for several weeks, along with our Unknown Blues Band-mate, tenor sax player/vocalist Big Joe Burrell. In doing so, we were building on the musical foundation we had laid six years before, touring with harmonica legend Paul Butterfield.

Those tours with Paul—during which we criss-crossed the US and played festivals dates abroad—presented us with the perfect opportunity to fine-tune our mix of musical styles and meld them into a cohesive performance. Each night, we would open the show playing our original funk and R&B-tinged jazz material, before turning on a dime to morph into a Chicago blues band when Paul came on stage. Audiences were momentarily puzzled, then appreciative, then fully thrilled at the show's sudden transformation from a "jazz performance" into a hard-driving resurrection of the legendary Paul Butterfield Blues Band.

Those skills we sharpened while touring with Butter really came in handy on our Russian tour. Our Kilimanjaro material went over even better with Russian audiences than we generally had experienced in the US—perhaps due to the long legacy of classical music tradition there, which had attuned Russian ears to virtuosic instrumental music.

But bringing Big Joe out on stage after playing our Kilimanjaro material proved to be the icing on the cake. At every stop, we experienced audiences palpably soul-starved for the quintessentially American music we brought with us from the other side of the world. Being part of the delirious excitement of those shows represented an enormous highlight of an amazing tour.

From a purely musical standpoint, it was a fabulously memorable trip—one which none of us will ever forget. But from a purely cultural standpoint, our brief glimpse into a society on the very brink of emergence from behind the "Iron Curtain" was a deeply puzzling, truly head-spinning experience.

In the months prior to the trip, we had been prepped by previous visitors to expect a country far more "third world" in character than we had been led to imagine, while growing up in the Cold War era. And once we were actually on the ground there, those third world descriptions appeared remarkably apt.

The sight of people in cities preparing for winter by daubing mud on the edges of their windowpanes was only one of many shocking reminders of a general level of poverty and technological primitivism we saw everywhere we traveled.

The splendor of St. Basil's Cathedral in Moscow was staggering—and must have been even more so to the peasant who made a pilgrimage there in the 16th century—but made for a vivid contrast with the rickety World War II-era trucks that filled the streets nearby. The three million priceless artworks and historical artifacts on display in the thousand-plus rooms of the State Hermitage Museum were utterly awe-inspiring. But a few blocks away, downtown streets were filled with shops containing only three or four items—motor oil, pickled herring, and canning jars one day … to be followed days later by tinned sardines, bags of flour, filter-less cigarettes and a small number of Mozambique grapefruits.

We visited luxury hotels in major cities, where the numbers of stairs between each floor was never the same. And often, not even integers. So, 15⅜ stairs between the first and second floors, 16½ between the second and third, and so on.

How did this happen? Because apparently, everything built in the USSR, whether a picture frame, a car, a luxury hotel, or a MIG-29 fighter jet, was built as a "one-off." Every one of them a Faberge egg, meticulously crafted out of nonuniform materials by hand—so no two were ever the same.

I couldn't help but reflect on a book by Tolstoy that I once read long ago in a University of Chicago history class. His thesis was that to understand Russia, one must understand that the Industrial Revolution that so shaped the Western World apparently never occurred there. And here, right in front of us, and seemingly everywhere we looked, was the proof. As near as we could tell, there wasn't a two-by-four, a table saw, a tin of window putty, or a tube of caulking on the entire continent.

All of this was mind-boggling to us. Back home in the States, we were accustomed to supermarkets routinely filled with twenty-five varieties of breakfast cereal and fifteen different brands of toilet paper. To skyscraper hotels and office buildings, where if you got off at the wrong floor, you wouldn't realize your mistake without a floor number tipping you off. To auto parts stores where you simply specified the year, make, and model of your car, and a set of replacement windshield wipers was pulled off the shelf and plopped down on the counter in front of you. In short—to all of the mass-produced abundance that Eli Whitney and his cotton gin left us as his legacy to our culture.

But here we were now, in Russia—the country that we had supposedly been neck-and-neck with in a nuclear arms race to Armageddon; a country where thousands of nuclear missiles were stored in silos, poised to strike the US at the push of a button— but where car owners needed to painstakingly repair the broken windshield wipers on their cars, due to the impossibility of finding replacements.

It wasn't only technological differences between the two countries that struck us, though. Equally stunning were the immense differences between how our Russian musical counterparts regarded their lives and careers, and how we Americans viewed ours.

One evening, I was having dinner with a fellow guitarist named Stanislav in his small but lovely apartment in Yaroslavl. He and his wife had literally hoarded ingredients for months, in order to prepare the lovely meal we enjoyed—a custom common to Russians everywhere we went. In our brave attempts to surmount our language barrier, we spoke about the music we both loved to play, the love/hate relationship we both had with practicing, and the never-ending struggle to fulfill one's potential.

At one point, Stanislav's face took on an anguished expression as he revealed his disappointment at being unable to make a living playing jazz in Russia. Wishing to demonstrate sympathy and solidarity with a fellow player, I said, "But Stanislav … in MY country I'm ALSO unable to make a living playing jazz." Stanislav was utterly thunderstruck by this news. "But … but," he sputtered, "But … how can that be? Jazz is such beautiful music. And America is the BIRTHPLACE of jazz!"

Apparently the expression "A prophet is not without honor, except in his own hometown" never made it to Yaroslavl.

To me, and to everyone that I've ever met in my profession, the notion that things are generally more valued in a setting where they are rare—and less valued where they seem familiar and "dime a dozen"—is so ingrained as to be unconscious. Every kid who's traded baseball cards and marbles or collected stamps learns that truism in one way or another from an early age. Or perhaps I should say "every kid in OUR culture"— because the basic tenets of a market economy are only relevant in a society in which there IS a market economy.

The intuitive understandings and lessons that one receives from setting up a lemonade stand, mowing the neighbors' lawns, or making one's weekly allowance last until next Saturday are things every American kid takes for granted—until one visits a culture in which all forms of personal or financial autonomy are foreign.

So, where do ya start?

As I struggled to find words, Stanislav impatiently said, "So, Paul. Can you tell me how I can make a better living as a musician here?"

At that point, overwhelmed by what I felt to be the impossibility of imparting a lifetime of experience in a few sentences of pigeon-Russian, I said, "Look, Stanislav. I'm just a musician. I'm not a businessman."

At that moment, I suddenly realized that the words I had just uttered were a monstrous lie. Not an INTENTIONAL lie. But a lie, nonetheless. Because in reality— for better or worse, like it or not, during each day of my life—I make dozens of business decisions.

Should I take this gig that was just offered me? Or should I hold off committing, in hopes that something else better might come along? Should I invest in a new piece of gear, in hopes that it will enable me to pay the investment back in better paying gigs? Will the money I spend on recording a new CD ultimately make its way back to me through sales at gigs? How long before that happens? And can I afford NOT to make that gamble? And countless other "fork in the road" decisions that represent normal life for everyone in our culture—but were utterly foreign to Stanislav, and to everyone he knew.

Again, another huge eye-opener about the culture we now were in the midst of. And equally importantly, if not more so, the culture we lived in back home.

At this point in the story, I'd like to briefly describe a specific incident on our trip, and how that incident caused me to reflect on my own cultural assumptions as an American.

Our band was returning to our hotel from a show we had just played in Moscow. It was late, and the long day of travel, load-in, setup, playing, tear-down, and pack-up had left us all quite hungry. To say that food options were slim would be yet another under-statement—and at that time of night, appeared nonexistent. Any and all entreaties to our translator/guide Tanya as to food options were met with stern disapproval—as if the mere desire to eat something at that time of night was a sign of moral depravity.

While rounding a corner, in a dark wooded area close to our hotel, we spied the flickering light of an open fire coming from what looked like a sawed-off barrel. A few people were huddled around the flames, poking at something. We asked Tanya what it was we were seeing, and she responded with disgust, "Oh, those Georgians. Probably selling shashlik." Hungry musicians that we were, when sensing the possibility of a flame-broiled late-night bite, we all shouted, "Yes! Let's turn around and go back there!"

But Tanya would have none of it … explaining in a condescending tone that "those people" should be ashamed of themselves. For Tanya, the scene we were hungrily eyeing—men cooking chunks of meat over an open fire to tempt the hungry appetites of passersby—was not the admirable venture that we saw it as, through the lens of our own entrepreneurial traditions. Through her eyes, the whole scene was a sad example of moral turpitude—emblematic of how low some people will go to take advantage of their fellow man's weakness. It was one of many glimpses our trip offered into the cultural assumptions of our Russian hosts, and by extension, the cultural assumptions of us Americans.

In relating this story to friends upon our return to the US, I realized that Tanya's response to the shashlik peddlers bewildered them, as well. "Why was she so unwilling to stop?" they asked. "Was it because she disliked Georgians?"

Well, in part, yes. But probably no more than many nations' sentiment towards their swarthier, earthier immigrant populations farther south.

"But why was she so disapproving of the idea of selling food late at night?" That one was a bit more difficult to explain, and my attempt at explanation was at best a speculation into the difference between the Russian and American psyche.

Tanya, it seemed, viewed hunger as inevitable—a regrettable but unavoidable part of the human condition. When viewed through that lens, anyone who was ethically challenged enough to "pander" to a musician's hunger at this ungodly hour of night must surely be an awful person. "Sure, people get hungry," so the thinking presumably went. "But it's immoral to EXPLOIT that hunger for money."

With our stomachs grumbling loudly, this slant on the ethics of selling BBQ meat at night was obtuse to us, and appeared equally foreign to the friends who I related the story to afterwards.

In attempting to make the Russian cultural assumption a bit more clear to my friends, I tried to play devil's advocate and said, "Look. In our culture, we have doctors who care for the sick and injured, and drug companies who manufacture pain-killing drugs to be used in those instances. If a patient breaks their leg, we expect that a doctor will provide appropriate medical care and prescribe painkillers for as long as necessary. Those doctors are paid handsomely for their services and expertise, as are the drug manufacturers for their products. And our society has no criticism of either of 'em in that case."

Warming to my devil's mission, I said, "But there ALSO are unscrupulous doctors who prescribe painkillers frivolously to patients willing to pay. And drug companies who are all too willing to encourage the practice, in order to line their pockets." I name-checked familiar icons like Hank Williams, Elvis, and Jerry Lee Lewis—and more recently, Michael Jackson and Eminem—wealthy musicians who developed recreational opioid addictions, and whose "do-re-mi" enabled them to find unscrupulous doctors willing to exploit their need for the drugs these doctors provided.

In the case of THOSE doctors (and the drug manufacturers who eagerly supplied them) our society directs a GREAT DEAL of criticism their way. Because in THOSE cases, these musicians were EXPLOITED by the entire system of "legal" drug peddlers—enablers all, whose moral code was overridden by their desire to line their pockets with money.

In looking back on my attempts at devil's advocacy with my friends: Was my drug analogy a valid lens through which to view the ethical implications of making money off another's habit, or hunger? And does the slippery slope of our own culture's attitude towards medical exploitation help to understand a bit more about Tanya's disapproval of the Georgians' barrel of shashlik?

Well, not for me and my bandmates, at the time the event occurred. At the time, we were simply hungry musicians, looking for a late-night bite in a country that seemed to regard us as morally on par with Elvis, rummaging through his doctor's kit-bag for another diet pill.

It's been observed many times, by people far sharper than me, that traveling teaches one not only about the culture of the place being visited, but also about one's OWN culture back home. And in my own travel experiences, I've found that to be totally on point.

Our two weeks in Russia left us with lasting takeaways—the wonderful enthusiasm of the audiences to our music, the touching hospitality we enjoyed in our new friends' homes despite their material wants, and the deep levels of repression that the Soviet system had used to control its people.

But the most profound takeaway for us was our realization of how quintessentially AMERICAN we supposedly counter-cultural, worldly-wise musicians turned out to be. Our attitudes, our values, our expectations of people and of life itself were just like our music—completely shaped by the American experience, in ways we weren't aware of before our trip.

Our American culture has found endless ways to supply flame-broiled meats to hungry musicians, late at night, at remarkably affordable prices. But supplying ways to understand one's own national psyche? For that, ya need to get outside the lens of your own culture, and travel the world.

I'll never forget the things we saw and the people we met on our 1991 trip to Russia.

Killin' The Blues ...

THE MOST BIZARRE RECORDING SESSION IN HISTORY

Here in Vermont, late October is generally known as "sticks season." The beautiful fall foliage that draws visitors to our state has mostly gone by, replacing the fiery autumn colors with shades of brown, set off by gray skies. The dropping temperatures—which were responsible for turning the lush green of Vermont summer into fiery reds and oranges, before finally killing the leaves outright—serve as Vermonters' warning notice that winter snows are just around the corner.

However, late October 2023 was different. It was a lot warmer, for one thing—and therefore, still possible to sit comfortably in a sunny spot on the back porch and pick some guitar. I was doing exactly that, when I heard the familiar "ding" of an incoming email on my open laptop, and I pivoted to see if it was just the usual junk, or something actually worth paying attention to. In this case, it WAS worth paying attention to—

NORMAN DAYRON SESSIONS—WEDNESDAY DECEMBER 6, THURSDAY DECEMBER 7, AND FRIDAY DECEMBER 8

—shouted the "all-caps" of the subject line. Once I got past the headline, the body of the email read like a press release, with floridly padded bios of the musicians evidently being hired for the session.

First, there was Charlie Musselwhite, the much-admired blues harmonica veteran—a man who moved from the small town of Kosciusko, Mississippi to the South Side of Chicago, where he cemented his reputation, before moving to California in the early '70s.

Next, there was Del Rey, who was described as "one of the finest blues slide ukulele maestros in the world." Now I've met Del, and knew that she was indeed no slouch on a number of instruments—but this description WAS certainly an odd one.

Then, there was me. WAIT. WHAAT? Had I forgot about a session that I was hired to play on, coming up in just a month?

The hyped-up description of my career was, strictly speaking, accurate—but did Norman actually think that it was acceptable to hire someone by simply sending him an email with his puffed-up bio on the personnel list? Without even asking whether he was unbooked and free to fly to the West Coast for a week?

Well, I guess in order for you to answer that, you'd need to know a bit more about producer, blues documentarian, and controversial music business figure Norman Dayron. So, let's hop in the ole' time machine and set the dial back to 1967—the year that I began playing in a blues/R&B band on the South Side of Chicago, centered around a harp player/vocalist named Jeff Carp.

Like many groups at the time, Jeff's band went through a number of personnel changes before coalescing in 1968 as a large, well-rehearsed unit of top-notch players—including the large horn section that I described earlier, in my piece on the making of "I Ain't Superstitious." The band eventually caught the eye of several music figures, including Dayron, who had managed to wangle a job as assistant engineer at the legendary Chess Studios—home to bluesmen like Howlin' Wolf, Muddy Waters, and other major players on the Chicago blues scene.

Norman was extremely impressed by the blues-based sound of our group, but had more commercial ambitions in mind for us. Since our horn section seemed to place us in the category of bands like Blood, Sweat and Tears and Chicago—who were quite in vogue at the time—he arranged for us to sneak in late at night at Chess to record eight or so of our original songs, in hopes of securing a record contract with a large mainstream record company in New York.

So far, so good.

The sticking point came, however, when Norman pitched his idea to us for the band "concept."

Chicago's South Side—already a tough place during the 1960s—had become a tinderbox in the days after Martin Luther King's assassination in April, '68. And the turbulence surrounding the Democratic National Convention in August of that year created an even tenser vibe on the streets of the city. So, when Norman insisted that he wanted us to seize the political moment by modeling our stage dress after the local street gang the Blackstone Rangers—and to call ourselves "The 43rd Street Snipers" as a condition of his pitching the band to record companies—well, that felt to us like an offensively inflammatory, gratuitously exploitative, jive-ass marketing scam.

In other words, classic Dayron. But for us, a bridge too far.

Though Norman's "extreme makeover" vision for the Jeff Carp Band never came to fruition, other schemes he hatched proved quite successful. As I described in my earlier piece, the two-LP set *Fathers and Sons* that Norman brainstormed was well-received, and *The London Howlin' Wolf Sessions*—which featured British superstars Eric Clapton and Steve Winwood—proved an even bigger commercial success in 1970 than its predecessor the year before. The fact that Norman hired me to play on both those projects—and was evidently quite pleased with how well my playing fit into the mixes—served as a small feather in my cap for decades afterwards.

By 1971, however, I was ready for a change. And sure enough, packing my worldly possessions into a VW bug and driving east—and then building a geodesic dome eight miles up a dirt road on the side of a mountain in rural northern Vermont—proved to be just the change I needed.

Fast-forward 40 years, to 2011. I had just finished performing an acoustic blues show in the tony, upscale town of Tiburon, California when a guy comes up to me from the back of the room and says, "Paul—Norman Dayron. Long time!"

And right he was. Forty years IS a long time. Especially when one considers that I was now literally three times as old as I was when we last laid eyes on one another. So, a LOT of catching up to do—which we did over dinner and drinks on several occasions, during the following years that I performed in the area.

Fast-forward again (but only TWELVE years this time) to 2023, when my back porch guitar-playing was interrupted by the bizarre, all-caps email announcing the "NORMAN DAYRON SESSIONS." How to respond? I wrestled with the question before deciding on the blunt approach. I wrote …

"Nice hearing from you, Norman! But dare I ask. What the heck IS this?"

The reply was even more bizarre—though nothing compared to how things eventually unfolded.

Norman explained that he had come into a large sum of money, and that this project was to be his crowning production achievement—his last best effort, and his legacy. And he NEEDED me to be part of it.

In return for my clearing the deck of all my prior commitments for the time, he would send me first-class round-trip tickets to SFO and put me up in the most luxurious hotel in Tiburon, overlooking the San Francisco Bay. He would pay me triple-scale for my time in the studio—"the finest in the entire area!!"—and then proceeded to describe the specifics of the catered meals he had arranged to be brought in. He had already decided on the menu, right down to the "prime, thinly sliced roast beef sandwiches made with a variety of artisan breads like Acme sweet Batard and a large pumpernickel or brown bread made with cherries and plums and a cheese tray of brie, Parmesan, Reggiano, and triple cream French delight, spread on graham crackers."

And to seal the deal:

"Paul, if you think this is just the bullshit fantasy of some old guy who's gone crazy, you're gonna be missing some very good fucking meals!"

"Listen, Paul, I apologize but you just make me mad as hell when you don't include the possibility of miracles happening, and people showing up like their dreams. I believe in that stuff and I can deliver and you know it, so don't let me down."

Yikes. With a crackpot pitch like that, how could anyone possibly say "No"? But the weirdness was only just beginning.

Over the next couple of weeks, more emails. And with each new email, a new lineup of musicians. The original pianist and vocalist were no longer mentioned, and a new vocalist/songwriter was now part of the mix. The constantly changing names and faces were becoming unnerving. But … whatever.

Then, a new game plan regarding everyone's lodging. Instead of nice hotel rooms, a 12-bedroom luxury "villa" was rented, halfway up Mt. Tamalpais. The photos looked beautiful—but how would transportation work, to transport everyone to the studio in Sausalito?

That question raised a red flag, and proved to be the last straw for one of the players, who bowed out of the project. And even for those of us who were still game, the spectre of being stuck on top of a mountain with no personal transportation spawned numerous dark jokes about Jack Nicholson's family in *The Shining*—leading one musician to decide to rent a car for the week. A smart move, as I was soon to learn.

The next curveball came after I got off the plane at SFO and was picked up by the driver Norman had hired for the week. I had expected the driver to be Norman's assistant, Farrukh, who I had never met previously but had communicated extensively with regarding logistics for the week. But no, this driver was filling in for Farrukh, as Farrukh himself was suddenly unable to do the airport pickups. Again … whatever. But another unsettling switcheroo, whose significance became clearer over the next 48 hours.

I decided that I should call Norman to assure him that I had arrived and was on the way to the villa on Mt. Tam. Before I could get a word out, Norman said, "OK. This is very, very important, Paul. So listen carefully. You are going to be the producer on this project, and I want the two of us to get together and negotiate your pay package commensurate with … "

"WHOA! Hold up a sec! I never signed on to being the PRODUCER of this project! I don't even know what this project IS! This is getting WAY too crazy … ," I found myself yelling into the phone.

But as I was soon to find out, I hadn't even begun to plumb the depths of the crazy that would happen over the next 72 hours.

The exchange with Norman had gotten fairly loud and ended somewhat abruptly. I put down the phone, took a deep breath, and exhaled to release the tension that had suddenly descended like a heavy weight over the otherwise lovely California afternoon. I suppose my exhalation must have been pretty audible—because Farrukh's friend, who had clearly heard the entire conversation, said quietly, "Yeah, things have been a bit weird over the last week." I asked him what exactly he was referring to, and got a horrifying litany of personal assistants, caregivers, and drivers being verbally abused, quitting, and then being rehired at twice the hourly rate they had been getting previously.

I said cautiously, "Wow, that sounds rough. But at least you're getting paid decently, after all that?" As if to emphasize the extremity of the situation, he said, "Yeah. I'm getting $100 an hour now. Assuming the checks don't bounce. Like mine did two days ago."

There was a pause, as if he was reflecting on whether he should be talking so freely to a guy he had never met, who had just flown in from 3,000 miles away to participate in this project. Taking a deep breath, he said, "But I'm not sure if I can keep doing this." Another pause, another breath. And then, "Some things aren't worth doing. Ya know what I mean? No matter WHAT the money is."

Upon arriving at the villa, I was immediately swept up into a whirlwind of chaos—largely fueled by Norman's mercurial whims, and his contradictory demands of each person involved in the project. And, as I quickly discovered, there apparently were MANY people involved in the project. There was the villa owner, Anita, who not only managed the property, but worked as a professional psychic healer for large corporations and energy worker for private clients, including Norman. There was Jacques, a high-end audio professional who had just flown in to oversee the installation of a $300K sound system at Norman's house. There was Charlie's daughter Layla, a singer/songwriter who had arrived with her band of New Orleans musicians—many of whom I knew already, but had no idea would be coming. There was Joel, the studio owner, and there was Ted, the head of one of several video crews Norman had hired to document the project.

A veritable Gilligan's Island of reality TV-show characters, all thrown together like chemicals in a chem lab, in order to see what eventually bubbled out of the beaker.

Norman had insisted that I needed to come over to his house ASAP after arriving. But that would require Farrukh, who was evidently engaged in picking up Osetra caviar, gravlox, red onions, bagels, and other requirements for Norman's lunch.

As a result, ASAP turned out to be considerably later that evening—at which point, I instantly grasped the extent of decline that the human organism is subject to, over 12 years of the aging process. The Norman of 2011 was a relatively fit and robust guy. But here, now, in 2023, the living room of his small home had basically been converted into a hospital setup—complete with gurneys, walkers, trays full of medicine bottles, and various hoses and IV apparatuses to accommodate the fluid intake and discharge requirements of an 83-year-old body.

To my pleased surprise, my old friend Eric Schoenberg was also there, having brought several very nice vintage instruments over to be used on the next few days' sessions. Norman insisted I play each one in turn, and try to envision on which songs I might use each one. Gesturing to a pair of microphones that had been set up on the one side of the room not filled with hospital paraphernalia, I was instructed to run through some of the styles each instrument suggested to me, while Norman recorded the pieces on his ProTools setup. There was a 1929 small-body Martin, a Schoenberg Soloist, a cute little Martin 1-21 from 1892, a 1957 Guild Aristocrat electric guitar—a treasure trove of vintage goodness for a guitaristically inclined fellow like myself.

As the evening grew late, Eric headed off into the night, and the conversation turned quickly to the next day's session. Norman again insisted that I was to be the producer for the project—but with a new twist. He wasn't confident that the video crew he had hired would have all the right instincts for what to shoot, in order to truly capture the ethos of the session for posterity. So, he needed me to also take on the role of video producer. I laughed, and insisted that not only was I not the best person for that job—I didn't know the first thing about video production at all!

After I insisted several times that this was even crazier than his previous idea of my being the music producer, the conversation suddenly pivoted. Norman pointed to something a few feet away, on the dresser, next to a bunch of pill bottles, and asked that I bring it to him. As he opened it, I realized it was a checkbook. A similar request for fetching services produced a pen, and as the room fell silent, Norman slowly began to write in the checkbook. Very, VERY slowly writing in the checkbook.

After around 10 minutes, with hands noticeably trembling, he carefully ripped the check from the pack, and, wincing from the exertion, he began to reach it across the table. I reached my hand out towards him, to spare him undue effort, took the check, and looked at it in disbelief. It was made out to me—and the figure that was written above the "amount" line, in painfully crabbed handwriting, was $20,000.

I said, "Norman. This is CRAZY! You shouldn't be making it out for this much!" Without a word, Norman reached out for the check, which I passed back to him. Five minutes passed, while Norman carefully studied the check. Then, suddenly, he said, "How do you make that little design at the beginning of the five lines?"

Huh?

"You know. At the beginning of the music. That little thing. I don't know what it's called. But I know YOU do."

I went over to the recliner chair that he was folded into and looked at the check in his hand. Norman had written, as carefully as he could, five lines under his signature.

He said, "You know, in sheet music. That thing on the left side of the five lines."

At that point, it hit me. He was trying to write a staff of music notation in the tiny area under his signature. But he didn't know how to draw a treble clef.

I said, "OH! You're trying to draw a G clef? OK. I can do that."

By now, lost in the absurdity of the moment, and of everything that had occurred thus far in the entire project, I couldn't hold back the paroxysm of laughter that followed. I carefully drew the G clef and handed it back to him. Norman looked at it and shook his head.

"No?" I said. "That's not what you mean?"

I began to dread the prospect of having to write an entirely new check from scratch. We'd be here until four in the morning, at this rate.

"No, the design is fine," he said. "But it needs the dots."

"Dots?"

"Yeah," he said. "You know, the dots. I mean, the NOTES. It needs some NOTES."

I reached over once again, took the check and pen, and wrote five little notes on the staff. And for good measure, tossed in a key signature of two flats at the left-hand side, after the G clef. Norman was pleased.

Mission accomplished.

★ ★ ★ ★

Somehow, the absurdity of the check-writing exercise was beginning to swirl deliriously together with the wooziness of the extremely late hour—and the fact that I had been up since 3 AM EST wasn't exactly helping. But through the fog, a plan was developing.

Rather than argue futilely with an addled old man about production duties, I was going to take the check and overnight it home to Celia to deposit. And then, at the conclusion of the session, refund the lion's share of the check to Norman. It just seemed like the right thing to do.

So, after another 45 minutes of being forced to try on different shirts from Norman's collection (in order to properly look the part of a video producer on-camera, I s'pose?) I was finally able to get Farrukh to drive me back to the villa to get some sleep for the next day's session.

The session the next day began promisingly. By now, everyone involved in the project had witnessed at least one or two bewildering episodes with Norman, which then became grist for a constant joke mill. In particular, *The Shining* had been established as the meme for the scene at the villa—so whenever a lull in conversation occurred, a low-pitched incantation of "Redrum" would reduce everyone to helpless laughter.

A general feeling of camaraderie is the norm for most gatherings of musicians. Especially within the community of musicians who play music out of the Black tradition. And ESPECIALLY among musicians from New Orleans. So, during the time that the video crew was setting up their lighting and camera angles—and Joel the engineer was getting drum sounds and doing line checks on all the instruments—we did what musicians generally do in stressful situations. We had a bunch of impromptu, intuitive jams that cemented our mutual respect and enjoyment of one another, and of our upcoming opportunity to make music together.

But things didn't go so swimmingly once Norman arrived. There were annoying complaints and ultimatums on trivial details of video lighting, degrading verbal abuse of his caregiver in the control room, and continual threats to fire various people in his employ, followed shortly thereafter by effusive apologies. The eccentricities that I had witnessed the evening before had been merely baffling. But THIS behavior—although presumably familiar to every orderly at every assisted living facility everywhere in the world—was considerably harder to deal with. Especially in a recording session.

The next day was no better. The tantrums and threats to cancel the session became more frequent and unpredictable. One of the tantrums actually resulted in the video crew completely tearing down their gear and heading home. The next morning, after Norman had decided not to call off the project after all, a new video crew arrived to set up. Like the previous crew, these guys were diligent and documented everything—including a shouting match I had with Norman in the control room which, I was told, actually made it onto tape. So, watch for the behind-the-scenes psycho-doc coming soon to Bravo!

And yet somehow, through it all, despite the unpleasant dynamics and manic behavior, takes were taken and tracks were recorded—which, presumably, was why Norman had hired us all to come in the first place.

As I look back over the lengthy email chain for the session, I realize in retrospect that the title of the project kept changing. At first, it was called "The Norman Dayron Sessions." But by mid-November, it had been changed to "The Last Session," followed a few days later by "The Last Session of Norman Dayron." Then, a week later, "Truth Is Beauty—The Last Session of Norman Dayron"—a nod to the Keats poem "Ode on a Grecian Urn" and a reminder of Norman's background as an academic at the University of Chicago.

The significance to Norman of the various titles became clear to me in a telephone call the morning of the third day of the session, when he expounded on the importance of the latest title change, "Truth Is NOT Beauty—The Last Session of Norman Dayron." As I sat on the veranda of the villa, enjoying the breathtaking view of the fog meandering across the bay towards the Golden Gate Bridge, Norman launched into an erudite 20-minute explanation of the distinction between the Aristotelian and the Platonic definition of truth—and the even stickier question of where it can be found. At an earlier point in my life, as a student in the College of Ideas and Methods at UC, these terms and concepts would have held a deep fascination for me. Now, however, those once-weighty questions felt like diaphanous, empty shells, drained of whatever flesh and blood had previously given them life.

Sitting in the morning sun, I imagined Otis Redding 56 years earlier, doing the exact same thing I was now doing, just a few miles away. That image of Otis, lounging on a dock right across the water from me, helped to remind me of why I had come here in the first place. The healing power of music is an admittedly over-used, corny expression—but if there's truth and beauty to be found anywhere on this earth, it's in this thing that I've been lucky enough to do for a living since I was a teenager.

So here I was, sitting in the morning sun, experiencing some of the first truly pleasurable moments I'd felt since I'd arrived. As I did, I started to wonder what parallels might there be between the glimpses of truth and beauty that I've been allowed to access through my life's choices, and the ones Norman Dayron had glimpsed through his?

I suddenly remembered his words of frustration in his email to me several months earlier, when he talked about "the possibility of miracles happening, and people showing up like their dreams. I believe in that stuff and I can deliver and you know it, so don't let me down."

As Norman droned on about Aristotle and Plato at the other end of the line, I started to consider the possibility that miracles still COULD happen. Maybe Norman working out these philosophical conundrums through this peculiar exegesis was his way to climb out of the box of his own bipolar torment. And who knows. Maybe it actually WASN'T too late for people to show up like their dreams?

So, I let him prattle on, in the hope that his meditation on the highest aspirations of the greatest minds the Western World ever produced might have a calming effect on his own. Which it seemed to. For a while.

But later that afternoon, I had an exchange with Norman that represented the last, final straw.

Of all the participants who had been hired for the project, Charlie Musselwhite was the one Norman had known the longest. He and Charlie had known one another in Chicago since 1964—which meant that their relationship was three years older than Norman's and mine. However, somewhere along the line, in the years prior to the session, Norman had concluded that Charlie's wife Henri was the devil incarnate, and once this dynamic bubbled to the surface in the project, it took over everything—including the music.

On the morning of the second day of the session, Norman summoned the band, Charlie and Henri to his house. There, surrounded by assorted hospital paraphernalia, his collection of vintage guitar amplifiers and several rows of pill bottles, Norman held forth on his grandiose but increasingly nebulous vision of what we had all been brought there to do. At some point, the rumors that had been circulating amongst the participants about bounced checks and denied credit card charges got raised, and things got very tense. At that point, it was remarked that everyone was due at the studio an hour ago, and the conversation came to an awkward, unresolved close.

Later that afternoon, Joel the studio owner received a text indicating that Norman was planning to come to the studio, and it stated in no uncertain terms that if Henri was anywhere on the premises, the session would be terminated. Fortunately, the studio had a second floor, accessible only by stairs—meaning that there would be no way that Norman's wheelchair could make it to the second floor. So, Henri stayed on the second floor while the session continued downstairs, and Norman was none the wiser.

Crisis averted.

On the third day of the session, Norman wrote another email—this time, to everyone involved. He explained that he would be arriving at twelve noon, and again insisted that Henri Musselwhite must not be anywhere on the premises. If Charlie was going to attend the session, the email continued, he needed to be alone and not accompanied by his wife—or Norman would cut her from stem to stern with his switchblade.

By the time this missive was delivered, most of the session participants had taken to ignoring the various threats and outbursts, myself included. The thought being, if you ignore the threats, they'll basically go away and be forgotten. But upon returning with Anita from an errand I was running, I got a phone call from Norman, instructing me to stand by the door to the studio and enforce his switchblade edict.

By now, the craziness had gone beyond what I was willing to deal with. Before I could think twice about it, I was yelling into the phone, "Look, Norman. I'm not gonna be your fuckin' bouncer. You're out of your fuckin' mind, and I've had enough."

Fortunately, Anita was still in her car, so she could drive me back up the mountain. In the car, I asked her, "Did I overreact just now?" She said, "Absolutely not. You needed to say that, in the face of all the insanity." Which was helpful reassurance.

But … NOW what do I do?

It was Thursday afternoon, and my flight home wasn't until Sunday. I was now stuck on top of a mountain with no transportation except for Farrukh, whose dependable services, and his overview of the various people involved, had up till now served as a rock of stability in the midst of the constantly shifting sands of the project itself.

But Farrukh worked for Norman. So even given my friendship with Farrukh, I was in no position to ask him to abandon his paid duties—which were to be at the immediate beck and call and cater to every whim of his employer—in order to drive me somewhere far from the grip of all this madness.

And even if I COULD come up with a transportation plan for my escape—how could I extricate myself from the situation, without leaving everyone in the lurch?

The answer, as it often is, was to concoct a little white lie.

I wrote Norman a text, explaining that I'd just gotten word from Celia that she'd had a health scare. A test for cancer that we had hoped and thought would be benign now looked like it might not be. I explained that I was kind of freaked out by the news, and that my attentions were much more needed at home than they were here with the recording project. Then, I rifled through my Rolodex and tried to think of who I knew well enough in the Bay Area to ask a big favor.

Fortunately, I hit paydirt on my first call.

My friend Jim, who has a place in the Oakland Hills overlooking the bay, said, "Sure, buddy. I can be there in an hour and a half. Sit tight, I'll come and get ya, and you can stay with me and Karen until your flight on Sunday."

Words can't express the relief I felt when Jim said that. I felt like I was being sprung out of an enemy prison camp—and suddenly, that weight that had first descended in the back of my Uzbek driver's car was lifted off my shoulders. Such a wonderful reminder of the blessing of having friends when you need them!

Staying with Jim and Karen was lovely, as I anticipated. And several days later, I flew home to Vermont. By then, the weight of the experience had fallen off me, and I was eagerly anticipating my re-entry into my "normal life" of being a working musician.

But there were still some loose ends left to tie up—the main one being that 20K check.

After a week or so of contradictory reports from Bank of America in California and from my own bank in Vermont, the conclusive verdict finally came. Payment on the check had been denied due to the "irregular signature." All because of that silly music staff with the treble clef and the "little dots" that Norman made me draw below his own signature.

That damn doodle on that damn check cost me $20,000. I KNEW it was a mistake for a blues musician to learn to read music!

Thus began a wacky exchange with Norman, concerning my plan to refund back to him a substantial portion of the check. He was by now so horrified and contrite about everything that had occurred during the session—and so mortified over the amount of money he had wound up hemorrhaging through his profligacy around it— that my resolution to refund his money broke loose a tsunami of gratitude.

Now that his check had been denied by the bank, we both agreed that the best idea to settle up was for him to write a new check for the reduced figure and send it to me.

But what to do with the worthless 20K check?

Giddy with relief at both managing to retain a friend—and receiving a substantial amount of money back—Norman sent me a lengthy description of what I should do with the now-valueless check.

He insisted I should frame it.

After all, he said, John Lennon's doodles had sold for $70,000 at auction at Christie's in New York a few years back. This check would presumably be worth as much within a few years. He then proceeded to describe the exact procedure to mount the check, in order to put it up for auction.

"You should mount it on an acid-free backing designed to last 100 years, with a front mat of acid-free cardboard, tinted cream or black, with a chiseled, gold, and angled edge, cut out around the check, and using glare-free glass, with, say, a solid ¾- inch Ebony frame edged with 24 karat gold.

"Then all the air should be vacuumed out to make it air-tight and a special machine should inject nitrogen gas into the whole assembly to prevent the damage caused by the aging of paper from sunlight and UV light and heat.

"The frame should be made of glare-free glass to protect the check from aging from the effects of UV light as well as the whole spectrum of sunlight, and excessive heat.

"The frame should be a center cut piece of ¾ inch ebony with a thin 24 karat gold ⅛-inch wide strip bordering all four sides of the ebony frame.

"The back should have hardened eye mounting screws connected by two or three strong strands of museum-quality picture wire. That's the way to mount the check if you think someday you might want to put it up for sale at auction for exhibitions in museums and galleries."

Was Norman just riffing here, surfing on the now lighthearted mood that we had established, now that the horrendous ordeal of the session was in the rear-view mirror?

Or was he serious?

I don't know.

And now, I'll NEVER know.

Because six hours later, Norman Dayron was dead.

Shirley Caesar

The Gospel, According To Shirley Caesar

The date April 28 will always serve as a reminder of my most mortifying memory lapse. On that day, in the year 2000, I was at the New Orleans Jazz & Heritage Festival. That year marked my fifteenth pilgrimage to the Fest, and with each year, my sadness at the devolution of the festival became harder to ignore. I had been catching my usual favorites at various stages around the Fairgrounds that Friday, biding my time until Shirley Caesar was due to perform in the Gospel Tent. For me, seeing Shirley Caesar perform in the tent was an absolute must-see, and held the promise of rekindling the unique community spirit that I experienced when I first started attending the Fest in the mid-'80s, but felt increasingly missing as the rest of the world started discovering it.

I made sure to get to the Gospel Tent early enough to get a good seat. When Shirley hit the stage, the crowd's roar of delight and adulation confirmed that I was in the right place for my "rekindling" experience. Shirley's appeal to her churchgoing fans and followers was deep and powerful, and the theatrical tricks of the trade—which every experienced gospel performer has in their toolkit—were so interleaved with moments of genuine inspiration that one would be hard-pressed to tell where the tricks left off and heartfelt spirit connection began. That is to say, she perfectly performed the ritual that her audience was there to be part of. And that I was there to be part of, as well.

Around 20 minutes into her performance, at the end of a knockout gospel number featuring an extended praise vamp, Shirley said to her audience, "I want to ask each and every one of you in the audience a question."

As the last few "Hallelujahs," "Praise Gods," and smatterings of applause faded to a hushed silence, she said, "I want to ask you a question. How OLD is your mother today?"

I knew that this tug at the heartstrings was also a segue into one of Shirley's many "mother" songs, such as "No Charge" or "Don't Drive Your Momma Away" ... and, of course, so did her fans. Nevertheless, I was happy to roll with the obvious emotional manipulation, and reflected on my own answer.

As I did so, I felt a cold shiver. April 28. Wait a minute. Oh, my God! My mother's BIRTHDAY is April 28!

Let's see. She was born in 1920, so that would make her ... Oh LORD ... that would make her exactly EIGHTY YEARS OLD ... TODAY!!!

How could I have overlooked that??? And why hadn't this come up as a discussion topic in the last six months with my siblings?

And then, I remembered. After we sibs had all engineered a huge surprise party for her 70th birthday, Mom had made us promise that we wouldn't do another extravaganza like that, so she could always remember that special 70th.

Yeah, but STILL!! How could you forget her 80th, Paul?

Well, I eventually calmed down, and after Shirley's performance was over, I walked out into the sunlight, humbled by the frailties of the human brain, but rekindled by the power of the human spirit. With, maybe, a bit more appreciation for parapsychology thrown in, for good measure.

Mom left us on April 28, 2015—exactly 15 years later, on her 95th birthday. Thanks to Shirley, I'm sure I'll never forget her birthday again.

Appendix

As I mentioned in my preface, this book isn't, and isn't intended to be, a scholarly history of the music and the musicians alluded to in my essays. I have many friends who labor in that particular field and have produced fine work, which I highly recommend reading.

Here's a brief reading list that offers a deeper, more comprehensive dive into the bottomless well of music alluded to in my writings:

Books

Danchin, Sebastian. *Earl Hooker, Blues Master*. University Press of Mississippi, 2001.

Conforth, Bruce and Wardlow, Gayle Dean. *Up Jumped the Devil: The Real Life of Robert Johnson*. Chicago Review Press, 2019.

Govenar, Alan. *Lightnin' Hopkins: His Life and Blues*. Chicago Review Press, 2020.

Gustavson, Kent. *Blind But Now I See: The Biography of Music Legend Doc Watson*. Blooming Twig Books, 2012

Wald, Elijah. *The Blues: A Very Short Introduction*. Oxford University Press, 2010.

Wald, Elijah, *Escaping the Delta*. Amistad/HarperCollins, 2004.

Online

https://jasobrecht.substack.com
Talking Guitar: Jas Obrecht's Music Magazine is a Substack which offers many fascinating interviews and well-researched pieces on blues artists. Highly recommended!

Photo Credits

All illustrations by Lorraine Halpin Zaloom except where noted.

Page 92   Dr. John, the Night Tripper *Gris-Gris* album cover. Imusic/Alamy Stock Photo.
Page 100   John Lee Hooker. Pictorial Press Ltd/Alamy Stock Photo.
Page 103   Frederick Douglass. Wikimedia.
Page 104   Jimmy Driftwood. Presley Dispatch-FB.
Page 109   St. Brendan Illustration. Chronicle/Alamy Stock Photo.
Page 113   Bousfield School Kindergarten. Author's collection.
Page 120   Café Au Go Go street scene. MichaelOchsArchives/Getty photo #73989957.
Page 123   Woodburned portrait of Jimi Hendrix. Lorraine Halpin Zaloom, illustrator, by permission of Jim Marshall.
Page 130   Hank Williams. Wikimedia. Photographer unknown.
Page 132   Geodesic Dome. Author's collection.
Page 137   Big Mama Thornton. MichaelOchsArchives/Getty photo #74298174.
Page 138   Buddy Guy outside Checkerboard Lounge, Chicago, Illinois. Marc Pokempner, photographer.
Page 140   Bill Berg's '52 Les Paul Guitar. Author's collection.
Page 145   Allison "Tootie" Montana, Big Chief of the Yellow Pocahontas, Michael P. Smith, photographer © Historic New Orleans Collection, Acc. No. 2007.0103.2.122.
Page 150   Harold's Chicken Shack. Author's collection.
Page 151   The Unknown Blues Band at Discover Jazz Festival Blues Tent. Courtesy of the author
Page 152   Unknown Blues Band in Red Square. Author's collection.
Page 160   Paul Asbell with guitar on his back porch. Burlington, Vermont. Rose Lucas, photographer.
Page 176   Shirley Caesar. Bob Daemmrich, photographer/Alamy Stock Photo.

Paul Asbell

Paul picked up the guitar at age 12, learning on an acoustic that his father had already "broken in" while singing pro-labor and folk songs at union rallies and concerts in the late '40s. Entirely self-taught, he immersed himself in the music from his father's collection of 78s and LPs—records by Blind Willie Johnson, Leadbelly, Uncle Dave Macon, Woody Guthrie, and Jimmy Driftwood.

By age 18, he had launched his professional career in his hometown of Chicago, performing at iconic blues venues like Pepper's Lounge, the 1815 Club, and Theresa's. He played as a sideman for legends such as **Otis Rush**, **Magic Sam**, and **Junior Wells**, becoming a fixture in the city's vibrant blues scene. His career soon expanded to gigs, tours, and recordings with **John Lee Hooker**, **Earl Hooker**, **Lightnin' Hopkins**, **Sam Lay**, and **Pops Staples**. He also contributed to milestone recordings, including *Fathers and Sons*—featuring **Muddy Waters**, **Paul Butterfield**, and **Mike Bloomfield**—and *The London Howlin' Wolf Sessions* alongside **Eric Clapton**, **Steve Winwood**, and members of the **Rolling Stones.**

In 1971, seeking a "spiritual battery recharge," Paul relocated to rural Vermont, settling in the shadow of Camel's Hump Mountain. He built a geodesic dome and tried, for a time, to live "like normal folks who didn't live the music life 24 hours a day." But music was never far away. Before long, he rekindled his full-time career, performing across jazz and blues scenes with artists as diverse as **David Bromberg**, **Big Mama Thornton**, **Sonny Stitt**, the **Sun Ra Arkestra**, **Joshua Redman**, **Kilimanjaro**, **Big Joe Burrell** and countless others.

Beyond the stage, Paul has shared his deep musical knowledge as an educator at Dartmouth College, the University of Vermont, and Middlebury College. His past students include accomplished musicians across jazz, rock, and folk, among them **Anaïs Mitchell**, **Nick Cassarino**, **Elden Kelly**, **Luke Reynolds**, and Phish songwriter, guitarist, and icon **Trey Anastasio.**